The Human Science of Strategy:
what works and what doesn't

DR BOB MURRAY AND
DR ALICIA FORTINBERRY

Commissioning editor
Alex Davies

Published by ARK Group:

UK, Europe and Asia office
5th Floor, 10 Whitechapel High Street
London, E1 8QS
United Kingdom
Tel: +44(0) 207 566 5792
publishing@ark-group.com

North America office
4408 N. Rockwood Drive, Suite 150
Peoria IL 61614
United States
Tel: +1 (309) 495 2853
publishingna@ark-group.com

www.ark-group.com

Layout by Susie Bell, www.f-12.co.uk

Printed by Canon (UK) Ltd, Cockshot Hill, Reigate, RH2 8BF, United Kingdom

ISBN: 978-1-78358-382-9

A catalogue record for this book is available from the British Library

ARK Group is a division of Wilmington plc. The company is registered in England & Wales
with company number 2931372 GB. Registered office: 5th Floor, 10 Whitechapel High Street,
London, E1 8QS.

VAT Number: GB 899 3725 51

Contents

Executive summary

Research shows that 80 percent of all strategic initiatives by professional service firms fail to meet their objectives. This book is about how to make them a success. Strategy is, in the end, about people, and will succeed or fail depending on how well partners, employees, clients and others apply it.

Scientifically, there are several basic elements in getting human beings to adopt any new strategic idea, which can be encapsulated in four questions:

- Will it give me more certainty in areas of my life that I most care about?
- Will it give me more autonomy, more freedom, more choice in the areas of my life that I most care about?
- Will it increase the amount of trust that people have in me?
- Will it increase my value, my status, in the eyes of those that I care about?

Almost all of the strategic failures that the authors – Dr Bob Murray and Dr Alicia Fortinberry – have witnessed or researched have come about because the key stakeholders have answered one or more of these questions in the negative.

The Human Science of Strategy: what works and what doesn't examines the issues behind each of these questions and show how they form the drivers of almost all human decision-making and behaviour.

About the authors

Dr Bob Murray, MBA, PhD is an internationally recognized expert in strategy, leadership, influencing, human motivation, and behavioral change. Bob's insights are based on his wide experience in business as well as his deep knowledge of research in the areas of management, psychology, genetics and neurobiology. Clients include premier global law firms and mid-sized firms in Australia, the UK and Europe, alongside many Fortune Global 500 corporations. With his colleague Dr Alicia Fortinberry, Bob won the American Science Achievement Award and was appointed to head the Obama Administration's comprehensive national work stress initiative. Bob's latest book with Dr Alicia Fortinberry, *Leading the Future: The new human science of law firm strategy and leadership* (ARK Group, London), shows the potential impact of the new science of being human on organizational success. With Alicia he is also the author of the international best-sellers *Creating Optimism* and *Raising an Optimistic Child* (McGraw-Hill, New York). Dr Bob has lectured at Sydney, Melbourne, Duke, Tufts, South Florida and California State universities.

Dr Alicia Fortinberry, PhD (Organizational Psychology) has gained global recognition for her powerful, lasting impact on top-tier law and other organizations and leaders. Drawing on the latest science of human motivation and change, Alicia enables firms to shape strategy and build the right leadership, performance and diverse, cohesive culture. Alicia's clients include internationals such as Herbert Smith Freehills and Allens Linklaters and major national and mid-sized law firms, as well as many Fortune Global 500 corporations. With her partner Dr Bob Murray, Alicia received the highly prestigious American Science Achievement Award and was appointed to head the US government's comprehensive national work stress initiative. Their latest book, *Leading the Future: The new human science of law firm strategy and leadership* (ARK Group, London), guides leaders to apply the latest science to areas such as navigating a firm or practice group through rapid change, managing high performance teams, and understanding the needs and motivators of clients. With Bob she also wrote two international best-sellers *Creating Optimism* and *Raising an Optimistic Child* (McGraw-Hill, New York).

Introduction

We are all strategists. In fact, psychologists now say that we begin strategizing within months of being born. We manipulate our parents – especially our mother – to get our needs met for sustenance, attention, and so forth. Your dog strategizes in the same way to get fed, walked, and played with.

Before you go shopping or ordering things online you strategize – you make choices and figure out ways to ensure that you get what you want. You figure out the platforms to go on and the shops to visit. You calculate the amount you have to spend and weigh that against the people you have to feed, clothe, and look after.

Essentially your baby, your dog, and you all use the same biological mechanisms to work out strategic responses to the circumstances in which you find yourselves. A general does the same thing in planning a battle or a war. A CEO uses the same brain pathways to get to a strategic decision as does a mountain lion, or a mouse.

Strategic thought and planning – no matter how you define it – is a process shared by all mammals that have what is called "higher cognitive functioning" (and perhaps some that don't).

It's what scientists such as ourselves call a neurogenetic process because it involves both our brain and genetics. In this book we draw on the many aspects of what makes humans tick, including not just our neurogenetics but also our biology and evolutionary heritage. We call this "human science". The more you understand these insights from human science and their practical application, the more successful your strategic planning and implementation will be.

This book then is for everyone in business, in government, or any other organization who has to devise and implement a strategy and wants to make a success of it.

Why we wrote this book

Sitting in the Sydney boardroom of the global law firm Herbert Smith

Freehills, with a magnificent view of the harbor, Mark Rigotti, the managing partner, spoke to us about how he views strategy.

"It's not just about getting to an end goal, or even a particular series of end goals," he said. "Essentially, strategy is a continuous process."

Almost all the research that we've done into what makes humans tick, and what makes a successful business (which HSF most certainly is) confirms that he's right. We get blindsided by preordained outcomes, goals, and targets, so we lose the flexibility to change when circumstances change.

In English the word "strategy" has essentially two meanings. The first – and what people usually mean by strategy – is "a method or plan chosen to bring about a desired future, such as achievement of a goal or solution to a problem".

Rigotti is essentially saying that the idea of having this kind of fixed end-point to a strategy leads to poor outcomes – often made irrelevant by changes in the market, technological innovation, or by changing business priorities.

The second, and more pertinent, definition, especially in today's environment, is "the art and science of planning and marshalling resources for their most efficient and effective use". For this there need be no end – only an efficient process. That doesn't mean a long-term goal, purpose, or mission is irrelevant. Far from it. Rigotti's long-term end game – for the moment – is to make HSF one of the 15 largest law firms in the world. But the process – the marshalling of resources and their efficient use – would be relevant even if the desired, or even possible, outcome were to change.

An intriguing way of looking at strategy, which fits in very well with what Rigotti is saying, is set out by Milan Zeleny, professor of management systems at Fordham University. According to him, strategy is about what you do, not about what you say you do. Strategy is about action, not a description of action. All organizations have strategy, whether they know it or not – it is embedded in their doing.[1]

One of our favorite poets is the great Scottish bard Rabbie Burns. Perhaps his best-known work is the poem "To a Mouse", which contains the following lines:

"The best-laid schemes o' mice an' men
Gang aft agley,
An' lea'e us nought but grief an' pain,
For promis'd joy!"

How like about 80 percent of all strategic initiatives! The vast majority fail. Their goals, particularly their financial goals, are rarely reached.

We've worked for organizations throughout the world, including vast government departments, Global 500 corporations and major national companies, professional service firms of all sizes and a range of not-for-profits. We have observed and been involved in the process of strategy formulation and implementation at every level. We have seen the occasional success, but we have also witnessed an overwhelming number of failures.

That gives us a pretty sound understanding from a business perspective of why strategies succeed and why they fail.

On paper, it looks like most of these initiatives should succeed – the thinking behind them is usually sound and the data convincing. Most leaders see strategy through four lenses: the organization's financial performance, market opportunities, competitive advantage, and operating model. Usually they emphasize financial performance and market opportunities because these play a prominent role in the business case. We will be looking at all of these factors because each is important.

But these four considerations don't represent the whole, or even the most important, aspects of success or failure. The more fundamental causes are human behavior, our drives and needs, and the way we think and come to decisions. These in turn are the result of our psychology, genetics, and our individual programming through experience. Importantly in this mix are our biases, beliefs, and assumptions, most of which are unconscious.

The biggest reason why strategies don't work out is not that we don't understand business and market conditions, but that we don't understand ourselves.

For example, we have been led to believe that we are motivated by achieving goals. The truth is that we do our best when we are in the moment, caught up in and enjoying the process of doing, of being in the flow.[2]

As Scott Adams, the creator of the cartoon character Dilbert, says in his wonderful book *How to Fail at Almost Everything and Still Win Big: Kind of the Story of My Life:*[3]

> *"If you do something every day, it's a system. If you're waiting to achieve it someday in the future, it's a goal."*

And again:

> *"Goal-oriented people exist in a state of continuous pre-success failure at best, and permanent failure at worst if things never work out. Systems people succeed every time they apply their systems, in the sense that they did what they intended to do. The goals people are fighting the feeling of discouragement at each turn. The systems people are feeling good every time they apply their system."*

What Adams, Rigotti, and we agree on is that having goals is not the main reason we often succeed in reaching them.

As we will see, the process of working towards a goal is more important than achieving it. In fact, a successful strategic outcome can lead to a miserable psychological outcome. Subconsciously we know this and it's part of our design specs. The process we enjoyed is over, the system we developed – and took pride in and satisfaction from following – is over. Often, it's a recipe for depression.

The trick is to follow a process, a system you enjoy and believe in, that meets your needs along the way. The goal is then just the first step in the next phase of the journey and the opportunities it brings for more enjoyment.

Our aim is to guide all decision-makers through these issues, to enable you to take advantage of the opportunities, and avoid the pitfalls, that they create.

Our perspective

We have worked with a multitude of industries and governments for over 25 years. We know business. But we also know people. Alicia is an organizational psychologist whose research and specialization is in leadership and culture. Bob is a clinical psychologist and a scientist in behavioral neurogenetics. He also has an MBA, which, he says, proves his sanity. Together we have won a number of high-level science awards.

We look at the strategic initiatives in the organizations we work for from what we call "a human perspective". Our aim is to encourage leaders to view their plans, their decisions, and their strategies from the viewpoint of what we call "human design specs" – our motivations, our drivers, our basic needs (see chapter one for more detail on our design specs).

Too often the business of business is seen as separate from the "fluffy stuff" of human emotions and behavior. Our job is to get leaders to see and understand that this human "stuff" is at the very core of what they do. This is something that thinkers such as Richard Boyatzis and Daniel

Goleman have been encouraging business executives to understand since Goleman's book *Emotional Intelligence*[4] first appeared in 1995.

Often "strategic" failure is simply a failure to understand what really makes human beings tick. As we shall explain, this failure to understand leads to a large trust deficit between those who conceive strategy and those who are needed to carry it out. Frankly, by and large business leaders are not trusted by either their employees, their customers, or the general public.

For example, only 22 percent of employees strongly agree their leaders have a clear direction for their organization.[5] This goes to the issue of competence – one of the prime ingredients of trust. In our experience the trust deficit arises because the leaders got the "fluffy stuff" wrong.

What leaders will get from the book

There are thousands of books on strategy – just look at the titles on Amazon. Most are written by corporate leaders, professors in the MBA departments of large universities, or consultants of the McKinsey/Bain/BCG/PwC brigade. All, no doubt, will give you good advice, but few, if any, will look at the subject from the perspective of human science and what really makes strategy work.

We hope the readers of this book will get a much better understanding of the human world they live in. This will not only lead them to make better strategic decisions, but also to implement them successfully.

The reason, of course, is that any business strategy involves humans at every stage. They devise it, they implement it, they must persist at it, they buy the products or services created by the strategy – they are also the regulators, the politicians, the influencers who may be called on to pass judgement on it.

All these humans may have to be taken into account if a strategy is to be successful. To adopt any strategy without knowing what motivates them is rather like a football team going on to the pitch with no real idea of the rules of the game, or a restaurateur setting up shop without first finding out what food his or her customers like.

We will guide you through the systems, process and human science aspects of strategy and enable you to avoid the pitfalls that mindsets, human psychology, and neurogenetics put in your way.

The failure rate of strategies

Probably you've heard, or read, about the "strategy execution gap". The problems behind conventional strategic approaches are well documented, with a failure rate estimated at between 70 and 98 percent.[6] There are many reasons for this, and we have already outlined the key ones. A more comprehensive list comes under 12 main headings:

1. Humans are simply bad at strategy;
2. Failure of leadership;
3. Over-attention to goals rather than systems or process;
4. Lack of executive attention;
5. Flaws in the basic assumptions behind strategy formulation;
6. Relational failure at some stage in the process;
7. Failure to collaborate;
8. Failure to consult – especially with employees;
9. Over reliance on big data;
10. The executive bubble;
11. Lack of a defined purpose that the strategy links into; and
12. Failure to take culture into account.

We will examine all of these in the course of the book and suggest concrete and doable solutions to each of them.

The good strategist

We will also show what makes a good strategist and examine what we can learn from the best of them. We will look at their key mindsets and, crucially, how they go about the business of implementing strategy. Often – maybe mostly – the "best-laid schemes… gang aft agley" because although the strategy was sound, the way it was carried out was not. The best strategists are also the best implementors.

We will examine the issue of what is best to delegate, to whom and when. But also, crucially, how to see the successes buried in an apparent failure. Failure to achieve a desired outcome usually means that the successes achieved in other areas as part of the process are, often tragically, overlooked.

References

1. Zeleny, M. (2008) "Strategy and strategic action in the global era: overcoming the knowing-doing gap," *Int. Journal of Technology Management*, 43:1, pp. 64-75.

2. Stahl, P. W. (2008) "The contributions of zooarchaeology to historical ecology in the neotropics," *Quaternary International*, 180:1, pp. 5-16.

3. Adams, S. (2014) *How to Fail at Almost Everything and Still Win Big: Kind of the Story of My Life*. Portfolio, NY.

4. Goleman, D. (1995) *Emotional Intelligence*, Bantam NY; Boyatzis, R. (2005) *Resonant Leadership: renewing yourself and connecting with others through mindfulness, hope, and compassion* (2005), Harvard Business Review Press, Boston MA.

5. Pendell, R. (2018) "Six Scary Numbers for Your Organization's C-Suite," *Workplace*, 30 October 2018.

6. Hoverstadt, P. and Fractal, L. (2018) "Patterns of Strategy and the execution gap," presented at 2018 MIT SDM Conference.

Chapter 1:
Why strategies fail

One of the saddest things about strategy is that 80 to 90 percent of all strategic initiatives (however you define strategy) fail to meet their projected outcome. There are lots of reasons for this, many of them due to our basic DNA and our psychological makeup.

We're not a strategic animal.

In 2013 an international group of scientists got together and devised a strategy game in which individual homo sapiens (100 percent of those reading this book) and pan troglodytes (common chimpanzees, none of whom are reading this book that we know of) played against each other.[1] The chimps won hands down. In fact, they predicted their opponents' next move almost 100 percent of the time – way beyond the capability of humans.

Why should this be? The answer, according to the researchers, is simple. Many hundreds of thousands of years ago, humans traded strategic cognition (the art of competition or playing against each other or finding novel ways to avoid predators or catching prey) for collaboration (the art of working together to achieve an objective). Specifically, we invented language to make collaboration easier and more effective.

This gave us a huge advantage that enabled us to become the most populous ape on the planet.

Language and increased collaboration were our survival tools. Hominids of our lineage – *Australopithecus*, homo habilis, *homo erectus* and the rest – had become progressively slower, weaker, less agile, smaller of tooth and claw, and utterly lacking in camouflage. Sure, we'd invented a few tools but essentially our survival chances alone on the savannah were pretty slim.

For survival we became increasingly reliant on the other members of the band that we lived with. They could protect us, nurture us when we became ill or injured, feed us when we became infirm.

We also had to rely on another evolutionary trait that we acquired – very fast decision-making. To survive in the face of imminent danger we had to replace thought-out decisions with virtually instantaneous action. What we lost in the process was the ability to make rational, considered decisions. When faced with danger we didn't have time for it.

A chimp can quickly climb a tree or run fast enough to avoid predators or use his teeth and strength on prey. A *sapiens* can't. So, a chimp has the luxury of time to use facts and reasoning to decide what the prey or predator is going to do next. In other words – to strategize. We don't. We have to use emotions – mostly fear and reward – to make decisions *quickly*. Emotions are processed faster than thoughts in the brain, which is why our decisions are emotionally generated rather than factually based.

The decision, once made, is rationalized in the prefrontal cortex (what used to be called the "command and control" center of the brain) after the event. It's not made there.[2] Studies have shown that the longer we take to make decisions – to weigh the pros and cons – the worse those decisions are.[3]

Our design specs get in the way of strategy.

We recently rented a car on the Côte D'Azure. Every year when we do this, the rental cars seem more complex. Which knob operates the turn indicator and which the windshield wipers? How do you know when the brake is on or off? How do you turn on the emergency flashers? What does it mean that there is a trail of water coming out from underneath?

We didn't know what most of the knobs did, and our French wasn't up to the manual. So, we drove along with our fingers crossed.

Humanity at the moment seems a bit like that. It's hard to have a strategy for now if we don't know how to find a manual in a language we can understand. Only recently have we been able to really look under the hood of the multi-faceted human system and form some idea of our "design specs". How our biology, genetics, and neurology influence our decisions and actions. We have spent much of our lives collating this research and translating it into simple and practical solutions. Informed by our experience over decades working with individuals, families, and organizations, we continue to apply the findings into guidance for people looking to live healthier, more rewarding lives.[4]

In this book we'll be talking a lot about what's under the cover – our "human design specs". Our design specs are the result of millions of years of evolution. It took some eight million years to get from the common ancestor of pan troglodytes and homo sapiens to where we are: hunter-gatherers designed to live very collaboratively in small groups on the African savannah. Modern research has shown that the closer to their lifestyle we live, the happier, less stressed, and more productive we become.

Every living or inanimate thing – whether a steel girder or a tree or a human – becomes stressed if pushed towards its tolerance limits (its design specs). If pushed past them, it breaks. The tree is uprooted if the wind is too fierce, the steel girder breaks if the weight placed upon it is too great, a human becomes unable to cope if he or she is pushed too far beyond what they were designed for.

For example:

- We were designed to work 10-20 hours a week – but we work 40+;
- We were never designed to retire, instead to join the council of elders – but now we are often forced to retire and often die shortly afterwards;
- We were designed to live in small mutually supportive bands – now we live in huge cities or work in large businesses and suffer chronic isolation;
- We were designed not to have leaders – now we live in overlapping hierarchies, each with its individual leader;
- We were designed to live on or close to the earth – now many of us live and work in tall buildings without contact with it;
- We were designed to make decisions on the basis of emotion and relationship needs – not facts or reason;
- We were designed to have fun, to enjoy what we do, to laugh while working together – something most of us rarely experience; and
- Above all we were designed to be mutually dependent – the rugged individualist is a myth and those who seem to be the John Waynes of this world mostly have severe personality disorders.

The point of this is that the further we get from what we were designed to do, the more stressed and depressed we get. What's more, research has shown over and over again that we make bad decisions under stress, including, of course, strategic decisions.

What is human strategic thought?

Given all of that, what is "human strategic thought"? There are many, many definitions of strategic thought, most of which make perfectly good common sense. To a leader, they are very enticing, and almost all organizations have in some way tried to incorporate strategic thinking into their forward planning. However, in many ways science is throwing a spanner into the works and saying that strategic thinking is not what it seems to be. The current, widely accepted, model of strategic thinking involves, among other things:[5]

- A "focused intent", which means being more determined and less distracted than rivals in the marketplace;

- Being "hypothesis driven", ensuring that both creative and critical thinking are incorporated into strategy-making. This competency supposedly incorporates the scientific method into strategic thinking;[6] and

- Having "intelligent opportunism", which means being responsive to good opportunities.

These three mental processes require what psychologists call "executive" cognitive actions. These include decision-making, short and long-term memory recall, knowing and challenging conscious and unconscious assumptions and beliefs, focusing, and so forth. Pretty "heady" stuff, it would seem. Or perhaps not?

According to the latest research, these activities or characteristics may not be under our conscious "cognitive" control at all. Instead, they are the result of other, less recognized, biological processes. Our "strategic thinking" is, in fact, determined by our genes, our experiences, our emotions, and our neurochemical and neurophysiological make-up.

Also playing a part are the actions and reactions of the other major "brains", clusters of nerve cells that humans – like all animals – have in our gut, heart, and skin. Every second, all of these feed information into the decision centers of the "head brain", which remains totally unaware of the process. The brains of the heart, the gut, and the skin remember and process experience and collaborate with the orbitofrontal cortex and other parts of the head brain to form unconscious assumptions and beliefs that will be acted on automatically when certain triggers occur.

In terms of decisions – for example, being responsive to opportunities – most modern research shows that we don't make rational decisions in the way people have historically thought we do. We don't think, "Ah, this is an opportunity, I had better take it". In fact, by the time we have thought this, the decision to act or not has been taken. By that time, the mind (a term we use to include the sum of all of the various elements in our neurogenetic make-up) has very quickly gone through a number of unconscious calculations in answer to a number of fundamental questions. These include:

- How will this affect my network of my supportive relationships or those I want to include in that nexus?
- Will taking this opportunity make me more, or less, safe?
- Would the actions involved in seizing this opportunity expose me to any loss or social exclusion?
- Would taking this opportunity gain me status in the eyes of those I care about?
- What is the level of certainty regarding this?
- Will this increase or decrease the amount of control that I have over my life?
- What do I feel about this decision?

The conscious brain doesn't answer these questions; no "thinking" takes place. The "answers" are automatic and based on genetics and experiential memories. For example, the very act of recognizing an opportunity in the first place is genetically based. It involves the same genetic factors that make a person either open or not to new experience.[7] You can train someone who has that genetic propensity to be better at it, but you can't expect someone who doesn't have that genetic expression to be able to "recognize an opportunity", far less to act on it.

Science is very quickly coming to the conclusion that "strategic thinking", as a conscious activity that a person can put their mind to, may be like the yeti of the Himalayas – a myth. There are aspects of it that some people may be better at, because of their genes and their experience, but probably nobody will be good at all of the mental abilities that are attributed to the "strategic thinker".

How viable is human strategic thought?

Charles McLachlan, founder of FuturePerfect (formerly Chairman at the Academy for Chief Executives) says that all firms – even very small ones

– try to be "strategic" in a range of areas. And that, he said, may be one of their problems.

He told us a fairly typical story of a software engineer he worked with who saw a way to link up suppliers of raw materials with small-scale manufacturers and craftsmen more efficiently. The middleman – the wholesaler – would be cut out and both supplier and craftsman or manufacturer would make more money.

He didn't need a lot of customers since his operation was small and cost-efficient. He and his daughter were the only employees of the enterprise. He did the techy stuff, including building the website and creating the algorithm to run it, and she did everything else.

He was quite successful at first and his customers were pleased with his service.

The problem was, what next? He'd been told that he had to have a strategy to grow the business (you know the old saying – a business must "grow or go"), so he sat down and tried to work one out. He read lots of books and articles on strategic planning and got lots of advice from lots of people.

He thought of many ways that he could put his original algorithm and others like it to work and finally came up with a strategy and a business plan that included opening into kindred technology-and-web-driven enterprises including dating apps.

The strategy might have worked for someone else with more resources but not for him. In the end he was forced to sell his original business to a tech giant for a pittance to pay down the personal loan he had taken out on the basis of his plan.

"I've rarely seen a strategy that worked," says McLachlan. "Most of them are based on mistaken assumptions or don't allow adaptation and modification when aspects don't work, or circumstances change. And particularly in today's world, that's going to happen a lot. Plus, the larger the frame of the strategic plan the less likely it is to be successful. Conventional strategic planning for a small outfit can be a grand waste of time."

McLachlan adds that the biggest problem is that a fixed strategy tells you what to do, whereas business success comes from weaning out the things not to do, so you concentrate on fewer things that you know work.

And it's not only small firms that discover that. So do large businesses, governments, and even social organizations.

Mark Rigotti, the managing partner of the global law firm Herbert Smith Freehills, told us:

"For us, strategy is a process, an ongoing dialogue. We have a strategy (Beyond 2020) but it is directional rather than a series of To Do activities. We have a number of priorities, currently five, including a push into China, but we're aware that any one or more of these might not be the primary idea at any given point in time. Thus, we revisit these priorities every 12 months or so."

As we shall see, McLachlan's and Rigotti's approaches fit in very well with what we now know about human design specs.

Hidden biases

One of the most annoying human design specs is the fact that we are geared to make decisions – strategic or otherwise – on the basis of our biases. Many of our biases are what are called "hidden" – in other words we have little or no idea what they are. Often when they are pointed out to us, we are genuinely shocked.

We all carry hidden biases from a lifetime of exposure to cultural attitudes about age, gender, race, ethnicity, religion, social class, sexuality, disability status, and nationality – in fact, almost everything. As hunter-gatherers they helped us to make the quick, sometimes life preserving, decisions that we mentioned earlier. The problem is not that hidden biases are hidden; it's just that they can be both inappropriate and wrong.

Nikala Lane, associate professor of marketing and strategy at the University of Warwick, has studied the characteristics of successful strategists and strategic implementors and also the hidden biases of those who choose strategists and implementors.[8] Overwhelmingly, men are chosen for strategic roles. According to Lane, this is because those who make the selections (male and female) are biased against women. They assume that men are more strategic and more capable of forming and implementing a strategy. Yet her research shows that these assumptions are wrong.

Often when she points this out people are willing to concede that others might be biased, but "I know my own mind. I am able to assess others in a fair and accurate way."

We can't; none of us can. Other studies have shown that up to 90 percent of all our assumptions about other people are wrong in some way (70 percent of all our assumptions are wrong, as we'll be showing you).

Our biases are so strong that they influence all our decision-making, especially our strategic decision-making. Even when we know we have a bias, and even when we know cognitively that it's wrong, most of the time we are swayed by it.

There are ways to detect hidden biases but very few decision-makers take the trouble to discover their own. Almost all the corporate leaders that we have spoken to over the years claim either not to be biased or they admit that they have biases but claim not be swayed by them.

That's one of the reasons strategies, or the implementation of strategies, fail so miserably most of the time.

Uninformed implementors

One of the big problems of strategic formulation or implementation is that often the people who should know what is happening, or is about to happen, don't. Either they haven't been told, or they have been told in such a way that the message is confusing or misleading.

Professor Milan Zeleny of Fordham University has noted the differences in the language used by companies that set out to deceive stakeholders and those that strive to inform them. High-sounding strategies, mission statements, and vision statements are useless, he says, adding:

"There is an increasing tendency to treat talking about something as equivalent to actually doing something. The talking-doing equivalency is a disturbing and continually increasing phenomenon. New generations of managers, even the digital ones, behave as if talking about what they or others in the organization ought to do is as good and as important as actually getting it done. Digitally suave generations have a tendency to treat virtual reality as reality, talking as doing, and information as knowledge. Yet, all that can be digitized is only information and will remain so. Knowledge is not information. Flashy and well-rehearsed presentations have become more important than actually doing something."[9]

We have observed management in many organizations craft strategies and then present them in such a way that those who have to carry out the strategy are totally unaware of what they are supposed to do.

A clear example of this was a large Australian law firm that we worked with. They had a strategy encapsulated in the phrase "Become a world-class organization". To do this they were going to "consolidate our presence in the markets we are in and disrupt those that we aren't".

This was handed down from the Board to the practice and department heads who were told to carry it out. As one of them said, "We had no way of either understanding what this strategy statement meant, or what we were supposed to actually do to implement it. The net result was that, after over a year of very confused effort and little guidance, the whole idea was quietly dropped."

As Zeleny says, words are confused with action.

We see this often. For example, recently we listened to a group of leaders of a technology team in a major UK insurance company argue for hours over the wording of their strategy, which they would put the Board. When we asked them what it meant in terms of actions that they or the people under them should actually take to carry out the strategy – i.e. to make the words meaningful – they had no clear, or indeed any, answer.

The executive bubble

One of the biggest strategy traps of all is the "executive bubble". Executives talk mostly to each other – often confirming what the CEO (or senator, or department head) is saying – and very little outside information gets in. The net result of this is inflexibility and an assumption of infallibility.

As many studies have shown, as executives advance up the ladder, they begin to blur the lines between leadership, power, and influence. They see themselves as more intelligent and capable than those around them in the organization. They see people who agree with them as more capable, intelligent, and ethical than those who might disagree.

Leaders tend to forget that they got there mostly because of luck and circumstance – exactly like successful actors.[10]

The result? Leaders get affirmation from a small group, usually appointed by them, which inflates their idea of how powerful and influential they are in the broader firm. Their influence becomes constricted, and their leadership erodes. Some people overtly use power to accomplish their goals, says Pete Hammett, the author of *Unbalanced Influence*.[11] He says others become used to having tools of power, such as the ability to dictate and set agendas.

Over time, that access to power distorts an executive's influence in the organization. They may have the title and power, but their disenfranchised team members won't see them as an effective leader. Those with different opinions choose to remain silent or they leave and take with them vital knowledge and ideas.

Executives who don't encourage challenge to their ideas stifle new ideas and solutions, and a strategy devised by groupthink will almost certainly fail.

David Brown, one of the most successful Australian CEOs, told us:

"A successful strategist must have a team bristling with 'crap antennas'. They must be free to tell the boss that his ideas are off the mark, that the strategy he or she proposes is meaningless and is highly unlikely to work. Unless they can live with honest feedback leaders are in the wrong job."

Bob worked with David for three years as he turned Wesfarmers Insurance from a write-off to a business worth several billion dollars. Not once did he ever witness Brown get angry with or disparage someone who disagreed with him.

The big take-aways

1. Realize your human limitations as a strategist. Humble is good!
2. Make your strategy about action, not words.
3. Remember that strategy is an ongoing dialogue, an iterative process.
4. Surround yourself with people with the guts to disagree with you.

References

1. Martin, C. F. et al (2014) "Chimpanzee choice rates in competitive games match equilibrium game theory predictions," *Scientific Reports*, Vol. 4, article 5, 182.
2. Bechara A., Damasio H., Damasio, H. R. (2000) "Emotion, Decision Making and the Orbitofrontal Cortex," *Cerebral Cortex*, 10: 3, pp. 295–307.
3. Kendrick, V. K. & Olson, M.A. (2012) "When feeling right leads to being right in the reporting of implicitly-formed attitudes, or how I learned to stop worrying and trust my gut," *Journal of Experimental Social Psychology*, 48: 6, pp. 1316-1321.
4. See Murray, B. and Fortinberry, A. (2004) *Creating Optimism*, McGraw-Hill, NY, (2005) *Raising an Optimistic Child*, McGraw-Hill, and (2016) *Leading the Future*, ARK Group, London.
5. Liedtka, J. (1998) "Linking Strategic Thinking with Strategic Planning", *Strategy and Leadership*, 26:4, pp. 30-35.
6. Liedtka, J. (1998) "Strategic Thinking – can it be taught?" *Long Range Planning*, 31:1, pp. 120-129.

7. Shane, S. et al (2010), "Do openness to experience and recognizing opportunities have the same genetic source?" *Human Resource Management*, 40:2, pp. 291-303.

8. Lane, N. (2005) "Strategy implementation: the implications of a gender perspective for change management," *Journal of Strategic Marketing*, 13:2, pp. 117-131.

9. Zeleny, M. (2008) "Strategy and strategic action in the global era: overcoming the knowing-doing gap," *Int. Journal of Technology Management*, 43:1, pp. 64-75.

10. Williams, O. et al (2019) "Quantifying and predicting success in show business," *Nature Communications*, 10:2256.

11. Hammett, P. (2007) *Unbalanced Influence*. Nicholas Brealey Publishing.

Chapter 2:
Purpose, meaning and values: why the why matters

From our Sydney office in the central business district, we look out over people striding, as the phrase goes, purposefully about their business.

We wonder, as we do when in London, Shanghai, New York or Sydney, how often they think about what they are really striding to work for, or striving for, once they get there.

It's certainly a theme of many discussions we have together. What exactly is our purpose, and are we fulfilling it as much as we can?

The purpose of Fortinberry Murray is to enable people to understand what sort of creature we are and to take actions based on that knowledge that will enhance the quality of our life, the lives of others and life on the planet.

Every organization we work for, from the global corporations and government departments and agencies to the one- or two-person law offices in small towns in New South Wales (where we are working on a mental health outreach for the Australian legal profession) has a stated purpose, usually along with values. These are most often tucked away in a file along with value statements, or perhaps emblazoned on walls that people stare at while waiting for the elevator and no longer see.

Some people we meet in our work do feel that their daily efforts matter, that they achieve something that has more importance than their individual wellbeing. Many don't.

But whether people ask themselves about the "why" of their endeavors or not, the question matters, not just to them, but to the success of whatever organizations they belong to. Purpose, meaning, and values – usually simply other terms for the same thing – are the fundamentals upon which successful strategies are built.

Each of the people passing by our windows is looking for meaning, needing a purpose to make their life significant, and trying to adhere to values that will guide their behavior. How do we know that? Simple: these are adaptive evolutionary traits and as such they are part of our genetic inheritance.

The purpose and meanings of purpose

As we have seen, more than almost any other animal, humans are social beings because our survival, for millions of years, depended on belonging to a small group of mutually supportive individuals. We had no other natural defense against the threats that *homo sapiens*, and other earlier branches of *homo*, faced. Around three-and-a-half million years ago our ancestors developed stone tools and from then on, until just 10,000 years ago, hunter-gatherer society remained basically unchanged. The difficulties they faced, which led to their genetically based behavioral patterns, remained the same. These adaptive behaviors – ones that were appropriate for survival in their circumstances – were selected for and became embedded in our genome.

Our concepts of purpose, values, and meaning – no matter how they differ from culture to culture – are essentially tools to enable better collaboration between members of our group, tribe, or business.

A shared purpose, initially perhaps to enable the hunter-gatherer band to evade danger and seize opportunities, deepens into a common sense of meaning and values as people develop their own language, rituals, taboos, and stories. The band builds a narrative about itself that strengthens and distinguishes it. Eventually the narrative serves as a guide to actions, systems, and processes – a strategy.

Strategy without purpose essentially seems meaningless – because it doesn't fit into our design specs.

The drives for meaning and purpose have a genetic base, and are part of what makes us human. For a group of any kind to flourish it must take into account these aspects of our design specs in its strategic, marketing, and other initiatives.

Seeing purpose in this context enables us to more clearly understand and articulate it in ways that galvanize us to action. It helps us distinguish the beneficial from the blah blah. We can get beyond the dictionary definition to the lodestar.

Purpose has, in evolutionary terms, several distinct meanings:

1. **Achieving short-term goals**. According to the dictionary, purpose is defined as "something set up as an object or end to be attained", or "a subject under discussion or an action in course of execution". Parts of our brain within the frontal cortex have become specialized in goal setting, but our goals tend to be short-term. We are far more prone, for example, to take an immediate, if smaller, reward in preference to the greater one that requires

waiting. Climate change is a graphic case in point. We protect current jobs and profits at the expense of our future. Humans up until 10,000 years ago had no need for long-term objectives except the survival of the band.

2. **Group survival**. Our other deeply ingrained sense of purpose is the survival, and flourishing, of the group, or groups, to which we feel that we belong. Emotionally these groups become like the hunter-gatherer bands our ancestors belonged to and we're prepared to make considerable personal sacrifices for their wellbeing. This sense of purpose is behind what firms cherish as "engagement"; however, in reality this loyalty is generally confined to a relatively small group within an organization.

3. **Social purpose**. This is what we often call the "mission" of the organization. In an individual we'd call it a "life purpose". It's usually directed at achieving a fairly generalized social goal. The reason for crafting a mission statement (you might equally call it a "purpose statement") is to inspire employees or members and sometimes outside stakeholders such as clients or customers. All strategic decisions must be seen to contribute to the fulfillment of the organization's mission or purpose. It's part of the "why" of what you do. The mission statement must be congruent with how the business is perceived. When it's not, the result is scorn, ridicule, and strategic (and often business) failure. Here are a few of the best mission statements:

    "To organize the world's information and make it universally accessible and useful." (Google)

    "To be a company that inspires and fulfills your curiosity." (Sony)

    "To create a better everyday life for people." (IKEA)

    "To create a world filled with unconditional love where pets and their people thrive." (Paw Tree)

Engaging with purpose

We asked a managing partner of one of the largest multinational law firms what he saw as the purpose of his business. Almost without hesitation he came out with "To create a large number of very wealthy partners who will spend in their communities".

If you believe in trickle-down economics (which few respectable modern economists do) this might stand up. But will it engender collaboration and engagement in a firm of many thousands, most of whom are not partners, or even lawyers? Perhaps not.

We asked our good friend Bill Henderson, professor of law at Indiana University, whether a professional service firm needed a purpose, or if excellence in practicing their profession was enough. After all, a lot of professional service firms – even very large ones – operate as if they were simply a collection of sole practitioners sharing real estate and ancillary services. There is nothing to hold the practitioners in these firms together except a collective drive to earn money.

"For law firms," he said, "purpose is a tall order. But even so, people need to feel proud of the firm they work for." There must be a reason – a social reason – for them being there if they are to feel fulfilled.

Another purpose of purpose is tied up with mental health. Some recent research has indicated that about 30 percent of employees in the US and other western countries suffer from serious mental disorders and burnout, mostly due to the prevalence of workplace stress.[1]

Working for a business that has a firm sense of social purpose is one of the ways that people can find resilience, and become more engaged.[2] Purpose in one's work is one of the prime bulwarks against both stress and its potentially serious offshoots – major depressive disorder and generalized anxiety disorder. The latter can easily progress to more grave anxiety-related problems such as post-traumatic stress disorder.[3]

Purpose and strategy

In a brilliant *Harvard Business Review* article written a quarter of a century ago, Christopher Bartlett of Harvard University Business School and Sumantra Ghoshal wrote: "Senior managers of today's large enterprises must move beyond strategy, structure, and systems to a framework built on purpose, process, and people. In most corporations today, people no longer know – or even care – what or why their companies are."[4]

In our experience, that is still the case. Largely because of that, engagement is low and retention of key people – especially in professional service and high-tech firms – is liable to be low.

The solution, according to Bartlett and Goshal: "Strategies can engender strong, enduring emotional attachments only when they are embedded in a broader organizational purpose."

A strategy without a purpose-driven "why" is empty.

What executives need to do is to capture their employees' attention and interest rather than try to get them wedded solely to the business' financial goals or targets.

It's manifestly not easy to define a company's objectives so that they have real meaning for employees.

In the 1980s, the late Bob Allen, at the time chairman and CEO of the then-struggling AT&T, realized that there was nothing in the corporation's strategy or "mission" that made sense to the average AT&T worker. It was too vague, too "corporate", too focused on things that didn't matter to anyone except the CEO, the CFO, and the Board.

He rewrote it to give the organization a very understandable, in human terms, strategic "purpose". His wording led to the kind of mission statements quoted above. He stated that the company was "dedicated to becoming the world's best at bringing people together – giving them easy access to each other and to the information and services they want and need – anytime, anywhere".

It was a mission – a purpose – that AT&T workers at all levels could take pride in.

But purpose is not just the purview of the person at the top, nor is it only important in relation to the business as a whole – it's the role of every leader at every level to provide their followers with a sense of purpose that they can relate to.

Purpose into practice

But formulating a purposeful strategy is not enough. Employees – and other stakeholders – must believe that it's achievable; that it's not just PR. Senior management must be seen to believe in the purpose, to put resources into furthering it, and demonstrate that making a profit is secondary to its achievement.

An organization that gets it right can benefit hugely.

One of our oldest and still one of our largest clients is PwC, for whom we work throughout the world. PwC's stated purpose is "To build trust in society and solve important problems". Most people know that there is a declining level of trust between business and the community, so a purpose to rebuild that trust strikes a resonate chord with both employees and clients.

Further, it's clear from the actions of the firm's senior management that they actually believe in the rightness of the purpose. The strategies of each of their divisions is aligned with this overarching purpose, and the partners can point to a whole range of actions that the firm is taking to further it.[5]

In this way, PwC's strategy and purpose are aligned. Employees feel that there is a point to their being there besides making money, and clients feel that taking their business to the firm is a worthy thing to do. What's more, according to many researchers, showing social responsibility in this way is a very powerful marketing tool.[6]

The big take-aways

1. A strategy must align to a purpose that answers the question "why".
2. Make your organisation's purpose clear, understandable, and appealing to customers and employees.
3. Make sure that all your targets, goals, and actions are aligned with your purpose.

References

1. Wigert, Ben and Agrawal, Sangeeta (2018) "Employee Burnout, Part 1: The 5 Main Causes," *Gallup Business Journal*, 12 July 2018.
2. Crane, Andrew et al (2019) "When CEO sociopolitical activism attracts new talents: Exploring the conditions under which CEO activism increases job pursuit intentions," Conference Paper – June 2019 Conference: EGOS 2019.
3. Mee, J. & Sumison, T. (2001) "Mental Health Clients Confirm the Motivating Power of Occupation," *British Journal of Occupational Therapy*, 64:3, pp. 121-128.
4. Bartlett, C. & Ghoshal, S. (1994) "Beyond Strategy to Purpose," *Harvard Business Review*, November-December 1994.
5. See: www.pwc.co.uk/who-we-are/our-purpose.html
6. Hemat, H. and Yuksel, U. (2014) "A Critical Review of Corporate Social Responsibility Practices from a Marketing Perspective: Is Cause-Related Marketing Really a 'Win–Win–Win' Situation?" In: Yüksel, A., Mermod, O. and Idowu, S. (eds) *Corporate Social Responsibility in the Global Business World*. Springer, Berlin.

Chapter 3:
The neurogenetics of strategy

If you want to know how to get the best from a new car, or a software program, or a "smart" hair dryer, or a bar of steel, you need to understand how they work. What were they "designed" to do, and what buttons, levers, or signals best stimulate them to do that? How do you make sure you don't misuse them so that they break? Perhaps you look up the manual, instructions that outline their "design specs".

As a result of an early interest in evolutionary psychology, Bob spent over a year studying hunter-gatherer bands in what is now Namibia. It was one of the experiences that led him to become a behavioral neurogeneticist as well as a clinical psychologist. He was fascinated by the biology of human behavior. How do our genes, our microbiota, and our other biological and neurological processes intersect with our experience, our upbringing, and our context?

Later, when he and Alicia began to work with businesses in the US and elsewhere, he began to explore the biology – the neurogenetics – of business decision-making, in sales, marketing, leadership and, of course, in strategy.

As we have seen, needing to have a social purpose in life is built into our DNA. But so are a lot of other things pertinent to strategy. In this chapter we will look more closely at how you can use the new information coming out as a result of recent research in the many fields of what we call "human science".

Humans are irrational creatures – that's the good news
From a strategic point of view, you may recall us saying, it's important to remember that a human is primarily not a rational creature – we are for example far less rational than chimpanzees, dogs, or crows. This is because our physical vulnerability ensures that we have to make decisions very quickly in the face of danger, and don't have time to weigh the pros and cons. Yet every creature with a brain structure similar to ours makes decisions, at least in part, on the basis of emotions – primarily

fear and the anticipation of reward. Currently there is no agreement among researchers as to what exactly constitutes an emotion. It's kind of "I know an emotion when I see it".

However, it is generally agreed that there are eight basic emotions.[1] These are:

1. Fear;

2. Anger (in its strongest form, rage);

3. Sadness (sometimes expressed as sorrow or grief, as when a loved one has died);

4. Joy (also happiness, gladness);

5. Disgust (feeling something is morally wrong or repulsive);

6. Surprise (being unprepared for something);

7. Trust (admiration is stronger; acceptance is weaker); and

8. Anticipation (looking forward positively to something; expectation is more neutral).

More controversially, shame and guilt are often included in the list.

Almost every decision we make is based on one or more of these emotions. Many researchers (including ourselves) have concluded that humans are not capable of making decisions on the basis of reason or facts.[2] Our strategic choices are about what we feel, not what we think; about what we fear and what we hope for, not what we know.

Because decisions are not made on the basis of some mathematically proven formula, every decision and every strategy can only be judged right or wrong in retrospect. It is justified, or not, by what happens after.

Does this make strategic decision-making irrational? Well, yes and no. Yes, in the strict sense of the word – it has no rational basis. But no in a more fundamental way. Since humans don't operate on the basis of rationality, it makes sense to look at strategy as something that will motivate employees and customers; that will make them feel emotionally satisfied in following you or buying your products or services.[3]

Or, if your business is your own, what will bring you the most happiness, pleasure, and fulfillment. And, remembering that we are process, not outcome creatures, that enjoyment must be in minute by minute experience, the ongoing "now". This does not mean that every instant must be joyous – every cold call, or tax return or 6am flight to catch. But a sense of peace within yourself, and times when you lose track of time itself are what the psychologist Mihaly Csikszentmihalyi famously calls "the flow".

Strategy, looked at in this light, is not about a specific business or financial outcome – because you may or may not achieve it and most of the time you won't – but an emotional result. Through the strategic initiative your aim is for yourself or others to feel a certain way and, as a result of the feeling, act in a certain way.

This is much easier to achieve and, if used well, will lead to a much better outcome. In a nutshell, strategy is about emotion-driven behavioral change, not specific outcomes.

Stress and strategy

One of the things we *do* know about human beings is that we make bad decisions under stress.[4] This is because when we're stressed, a part of the brain called the amygdala springs into action. Often called the fear center of the brain, the amygdala is also a repository of memory, particularly negative experiences, and controls such strong emotions as anxiety and aggression.

In his book *Emotional Intelligence* Daniel Goleman coined the term "amygdala hijack" to describe how in response to threat that part of the brain corrals the human nervous system into a flight, fight, or freeze response.[5] All the higher order cognitive areas of the brain are shut down, fast!

In strategy terms this can mean:

- That no coherent strategy emerges (freeze) – think Kodak and digital cameras; or
- A strategy that, in effect, makes the decision-makers of the business completely change their business model or area – even going into areas for which they have no history or expertise (flee) – think MGM and airlines, or Trump and casinos; or
- Involvement in competitive wars for no apparent reason (fight) – think America's trade war with China.

We have seen the effects of fear in many of our clients. The higher the stress level in the organization or of the strategists individually, the worse the strategic choices. A pertinent example of the flight effect and its results can be seen from this UK example.[6]

The owner of a well-established software development company feared that the business area he was in would soon become a red sea of competition and thus destroy the profitability of the business.

He took the decision to move from a pure service model to building software products. He imagined that he could take some of the existing bespoke systems that he had built and easily and cheaply sell them as standard products. He imagined that he had found a bluer ocean to swim in.

Of course, he would have to keep the original business going while he labored to make the switch.

Inevitably, the attempt to do this had a very bad impact on the company. The length of the sales cycle, and investment in product development, also challenged both profitability and cashflow.

In his attempt to give time and expertise to the design of the new products (which he found to be much more problematical than he had originally thought) and gain traction in the market (which could no longer be a one-man operation) he had allowed the scale of the operation to grow so that almost 50 people were now engaged in the business. This was way beyond his management experience or capability, and he became increasingly stressed. Once more, the amygdala seemed to take over.

The emotional and psychological toll had gotten to the point that, despite the fact there was an outline deal on the table to sell the new products to an established software house for a significant seven figure sum, he chose instead to put the company into voluntary liquidation. Just get out, his fear center told him, just flee – even though going ahead with the sale would have gotten him out of trouble.

As a result, all the investment over the previous four years came to nothing and the business was closed without returning any value to the founder or his other shareholders.

Sadly, the founder was not prepared to listen to the advice of either his finance director (a very experienced senior professional) or his technical director (who ran the software development activities) who could have demonstrated the value from the product sale.

It's all about relationships

As we have said before, humans are relationship-centered animals – we are totally interdependent, probably more so than any other mammal. The strength of our relationships determines our mental and physical health, our career, and almost every other aspect of our lives.

Yet for some reason when we look at strategic initiatives, we tend to put them in a different category than decisions that we make in other aspects of our lives. As we sometimes say, there is a difference between our "work" relationships and our "home" relationships.

And this creates problems, lots of them. We want our strategic decision-making to be somehow divorced from human emotions and biases, but it can't be. Recent findings have shown that even the most sophisticated AI has the "human failings" of its programmers built into it.

In fact, a strategic initiative can be seen as just another way of forming or controlling relationships.[7] These relationships can be with your clients or customers, your shareholders or your employees. You may think of it as "selling more products" or "improving overall efficiency" or "raising the level of profitability" but, whatever label you put on it, strategy is still about people.

A mid-sized private company that we worked with a few years ago wanted to reduce its office rental costs and devised a plan to move location from the central business district of Melbourne, Australia, to an inner suburb where the rents were much lower. It was a strategic move that made a lot of sense. The employees of the firm were told that there would be a move and, overall, were quite happy with the idea – especially as they were told that the new area had a lot of inexpensive places to go for lunch. They happily went and explored the area and had gatherings in local coffee shops or Thai eateries. Some even found that they could save on commute costs.

One day, two of the company's Board members discovered what they thought was the perfect location for the enterprise in another suburb – as close to the CBD as the first, but in their view much more in keeping with the nature of the business. It was, incidentally, closer to the offices of a couple of the companies whose boards these two gentlemen sat on.

Since there was an offer in the works for these new premises, the Board members persuaded the CFO and the CEO to make the switch.

On the face of it the new area had no inexpensive lunch places, no Thai eateries, and only a small number of coffee shops. And for most employees the commute was a bit more expensive. Many of the employees felt betrayed and the company, for many months, suffered a fall-off in engagement and had to cope with the attrition of some key personnel.

Over the first few months after the move, it transpired that the new area had plenty of restaurants, cafes, and a decent food court – just a little walk away from the offices (or a one-stop train ride). But the damage had been done.

What the Board members, the CEO, and the CFO didn't realize was that the issue was no longer about the neighborhood or the new offices or even Thai restaurants, but about the relationship between them as leaders and their employees. The workers felt that they hadn't been consulted, and that their autonomy had been compromised. Trust was broken and they no longer felt part of the same "tribe" as management.

We were able to resolve the issue by helping management to find ways to restore the relationship through finding ways to increase staff autonomy and status through involving them in other decisions that might affect their work. The important thing is that the relationship was restored.

Change phobia

We live in a "temporary society" with a high expectation that things will change rapidly, and not always for the best. Furthermore, the leaders of most businesses also believe that constantly introducing change can give an organization a competitive advantage in both the domestic and the international business environment. Yet this is so against human design specs.

Change is one of the greatest stressors. And too much change too quickly and without buy-in from all involved can thrust an organization into fight, flight, or freeze – or all three.

We know of one major financial institution that, in response to rapid changes in the business and regulatory environment, instituted a bold strategy to change its customer offerings, its ways of working and much of its staff over a short period. Nor is there any end to change in sight. The stress, which had instigated the first strategy, grew exponentially. Some groups became so frozen that overall productivity and output slowed to a trickle or stopped, and the rate of critical glitches far outpaced the fixes.

Prior to the Industrial Revolution, there had been very little real change in human society – for the bulk of our species at any rate – for ten thousand years (since the first introduction of agriculture). Before that there was stasis in *homo sapiens'* society for 500,000 years and before that for the millions of years since the first human-like creatures appeared. Resistance to change became part of our DNA, and it still is.

This is one of the things that constantly irks the leaders of any business. In terms of neurophysiology, change goes through the same pathways as physical pain and relational trauma. Yet every strategic initiative obviously involves change, since that's the point of it.

Why did evolution make us so change phobic? The reason, according to most research, is that we fear that any significant change will result in a disruption in our relational support network, whether that be at work or outside.[8]

If people feel that their important relationships are in some way under threat, they will resist all and every change. On the other hand, if they feel that their important relationships are secure, they will be much more open to trying new things.

We have found that strategic or transformational change is a balancing act and should involve the entire workforce (i.e. leaders, managers, and workers). Change initiatives work best if intact groups can be kept together – at least socially – in the workplace.

We have also found that if the reason for strategic change is just left to business leaders, the failure rate of initiatives is very high. In fact, identifying alterations in the internal and external environment, as well as introducing change, should not solely be the responsibility of leaders but rather of all employees in an organization.

If people *feel* (not "understand" – this is not about facts or logical arguments) that the change is in the best interests of their "tribe" – a group that they are committed to and from whom they receive support and protection – then the initiative has a high chance of success. Change is not static in nature but rather a dynamic and natural process linking all members of an organization (i.e. leaders, managers, and workers) together like a spiral that is kept under a positive, creative tension. What holds it together – the enabler of change – is the continuity of relationships within the organization.

When we say that humans fear change, what we're really saying is that people fear any disruption to their relationship nexus. In the end, any kind of substantial change, as Jeanie Daniel Duck, ex-leader of the Boston Consulting Group famously said, is intensely personal in nature.[9]

It only works if it solidifies relationships and commitment and doesn't work if it doesn't.

The big take-aways

1. Any major decision – strategic or otherwise – taken under stress will be wrong.
2. Take employees into the decision-making process of any issue that affects them.
3. To succeed in fundamental change, allow your followers to take the lead.

References

1. Plutchik, R. (1997) "The circumplex as a general model of the structure of emotions and personality." In R. Plutchik & H. R. Conte (Eds.), *Circumplex models of personality and emotions* (pp. 17-45), American Psychological Association, Washington, DC, US.

2. Naqvi, N. (2006) "The Role of Emotion in Decision Making: A Cognitive Neuroscience Perspective," *Current Directions in Psychological Science*, 15:5, pp. 260-264.

3. Herd, Kelly B and Mehta, Ravi (2019) "Head versus Heart: The Effect of Objective versus Feelings-Based Mental Imagery on New Product Creativity," *Journal of Consumer Research*, 46: 1, pp. 36–52.

4. Friedman, A. et al (2017) "Chronic Stress Alters Striosome-Circuit Dynamics, Leading to Aberrant Decision-Making," *Cell*, 171:5, pp. 1191-1205.

5. Goleman, D. (1996) *Emotional Intelligence*, Bloomsbury Publishing, London, UK.

6. My thanks to Charles McLachlan of FuturePerfect for this case history.

7. Neill, M. (2014) "Building buy-in: The need for internal relationships and informal coalitions," *ScienceDirect*, 40:3, pp. 598-605.

8. Stadtländer, C. T. K.-H. (2006) "Strategically Balanced Change: A Key Factor in Modern Management," *Electronic Journal of Business Ethics and Organization Studies*, 11:1.

9. Duck, J. D. (1993) "Managing change: The art of balancing", *Harvard Business Review*, 71:6, pp. 109-118.

Chapter 4:
Why the assumptions behind strategies are almost always wrong

"The explanation requiring the fewest assumptions is most likely to be correct."
Franciscan friar William of Ockham (1285–1347)

How our assumptions influence our decisions

A mid-size London-based law firm we work with, which has offices in various Asian countries, decided to more robustly centralize support services and strategy. They assumed that this would enhance efficiency and alignment, thus strengthening the brand and bring in more work. The strategy failed: the non-Londoners complained that the HR and BD staff didn't understand their local challenges, and the partners complained that their business was different in different cultures. Business fell off, and head office abandoned that approach.

How did the leaders, who were intelligent and had the firm's best interests in mind, make such a mistake?

To better understand why we make decisions (strategic and otherwise) that often turn out wrong, let's look at their biological basis.

The internal biological factors behind our decisions are many and varied, as the cliché goes. We're not aware of most of them – in fact we may not be consciously aware of any of them. These influencers include our brain (and not just the one in our head, but the nerve nexuses through the body that directly and indirectly guide our actions); our genetics; and our beliefs and assumptions. In the last few years we have learned far more than we ever did about the interactions between various parts of the nervous system and how they affect our choices.

In the head brain, one of the trickiest parts is the basal ganglia – the part concerned (among other things) with learned habitual response. The basal ganglia unconsciously compels us to do what we've always done, even when we think it's different.

"Gut decisions" turn out to be a very apt description. Our gut microbiota control many of our emotional states, which direct actions. Our "gut brain" makes about 60 percent of our decisions through the inter-actions between the gut, the microbiota, and the neurotransmitters that affect our emotions and behavior.[1]

Then there's the newly discovered "skin brain". Scientists discovered fairly recently that the skin organizes the formation of muscle tissue and largely dictates movement (and the ability to move), the decisions that lead to movement, those that flow from movement and, somewhat controversially, the memories that result from movement – such as shaking hands, for example.[2]

At about the same time, researchers discovered that homeostasis in the heart dictates a range of positive emotions and the decisions that flow from them. The head brain and the heart influence each other in many ways. Disturbing thoughts cause stress hormones – especially cortisol – to influence and even damage the heart, which in turn sends signals to the amygdala – the fear center of the brain – causing us to adopt ongoing threat responses that can lead to bad or inappropriate decision-making.[3]

Our genetics influence – at times dictate – our actions. For example, we are born with a predisposition to vote liberal or conservative, to be more or less risk averse, to be a detail- or bigger-picture-person, to be a follower or a leader, with all the behavioral and decision-making traits these entail.

Perhaps the most powerful influencers are our assumptions and beliefs. Some of these are genetically based, but the vast majority are learned, mostly in childhood. We are aware of many of our assumptions – perhaps 50 percent. We often we call these our preferences. The rest we're not consciously aware of.

Assumptions and biases

Biases and assumptions are everywhere and both, in some ways, are necessary. They allow us to make decisions quickly based on expe-riences. We are all biased and we all make assumptions. There is a difference between a bias and an assumption, even though they usually work together.

For anyone in business it's critical to understand your biases – your prejudices – and also what you assume about any situation. Let's start with assumptions and begin with a definition: "An assumption is any statement or idea that is not supported by evidence". It's a kind of claim.

Let's take a statement: "You ought to invest in XY Corp, it's a very profitable enterprise". Hidden in this are a number of assumptions about the relationship between you and the person giving you the information, and that person and XY Corp, both of which you rely on if you are going to take the information seriously. For example:

- The person making the recommendation knows what (s)he's talking about;
- (S)he knows something about XY Corp;
- (S)he's telling the truth; and
- You both have the same understanding of what a good investment is and what profitable is in this context.

In fact, we very rarely notice these hidden assumptions – even when making the most critical or strategic decisions – and even more rarely do we question them when we do see them.

Recent research has found that about 70 percent of all our assumptions and beliefs are factually wrong. Yet we rely on them in almost all decision-making.[4] We reject ideas and decisions that aren't aligned with our assumptions – even when we know that those assumptions are incorrect!

Imagine you have to give very negative performance feedback to a colleague with whom you've worked for a long time and like. You know that it's better for you and even your associate to deliver the message quickly and clearly. Yet you may put it off, even until events have taken the situation out of your hands. Many do.

Even when we think we're being totally rational and are relying on the data a computer spits out we will subconsciously scan the information until we find some item that accords with our assumptions and hone in on that as proof that we were right all along. We will then spend the rest of our "decision-making time" finding excuses for our judgement.

Many of our deeply held assumptions form part of our personality. Any attack on them – even questioning of them – can be seen as an attack on ourselves. This is true of even the most "level-headed" business-person or professional service provider. Our neurogenetic system is organized to treat anyone who attacks a deeply-held assumption or belief as an enemy – a danger to our ego, our very conception of ourselves.

There's no real difference evidentially between an assumption and a belief. The core difference between the two might be summed up by saying that a belief entails "feeling" or "emotion" whereas an assumption doesn't necessarily. We more fiercely defend a belief because of this "feeling".

People have gone to war over beliefs, but not, generally, over assumptions, although mistakes based on false assumptions have led to conflict.

Our strategic thinking is underpinned by our assumptions – and sometimes beliefs – about the situation or the people we are dealing with. The failure of most strategic initiatives is largely due to the fact that we haven't been aware of the underlying assumptions behind the strategy or had the psychological courage to challenge the ones we are aware of.

Our biases, like our assumptions, are pervasive and resistant to challenge. A bias is a prejudice for or against someone or something. Unlike a belief, it may have some "evidence" behind it, but that evidence is always limited or one-sided.

Being biased is the opposite of being open-minded or neutral. Someone may take the recommendation to invest in XY Corp because it is made by a white, apparently straight, middle-aged, middle-class male and reject it if it is made by a black, middle-class, apparently straight, female. Or anyone who is, or isn't, gay. Or accept the advice if it comes from a commentator on Fox News and reject the same recommendation if it comes from the *New York Times*.

All of these are examples of bias operating in conjunction with assumptions.

Assumptions prevent listening

One of the biggest dangers of biases, beliefs, and assumptions is that they prevent us from really listening to what people say. Partly because of our assumptions, beliefs, and biases we only really hear about 40 percent of what people say. By and large we are terrible listeners.[6]

Part of the reason is that we get caught up in our assumptions, and what's known as the "perceptual filter" comes into play. We start an internal argument with the speaker and invent reasons why he or she is wrong, thus missing the point they are trying to make. There are several other reasons why we don't listen very well, which are set out in chapter 9.

In a discussion about strategy this means that often the participants are not really listening to each other and any agreements they come to will often be interpreted wildly differently. This can make a nonsense of the whole discussion – as we have frequently observed.

For example, the Board of a major law firm in Australia decided, after much discussion, and after seeking the advice of one of the Big Three consultancies,[7] that their strategy going forward was to make the firm recognized as "a world-class law firm". As it turned out, everyone had a differing assumption as to what that meant, and this led to constant arguments and disputes. In the end they ditched the whole project.

"We had no idea of what was meant by 'world-class,' or rather we all had different ideas," said one practice group leader. "Our solicitors were getting conflicting instructions. Our clients complained that there was no unity of behavior within the firm and many of them went off into the welcoming arms of our competitors."

Overcoming your hidden assumptions and biases

As we said earlier, about 50 percent of all our assumptions are hidden. We don't consciously know most of what we believe, what biases we secretly have, or what assumptions we reflexively hold.

How can you test for your hidden assumptions? The only way you can reliably do this is to examine all the decisions that you have made over the last year or more. You will always find that there's a consistent pattern of decision-making that is the result of a hidden belief, bias, or assumption. For example, you may find that you have a tendency to avoid making decisions, even though you think you're a capable decision-maker. Now ask yourself: What would be the assumptions that a person held who displayed that pattern? It could be that "All my decisions tend to be risky, therefore I should not make any decisions".

Or perhaps one of the things that you consciously believe about yourself is that you're free of racial or gender bias. Almost all of us incorrectly believe that. However, one day your head of HR tells you that you have been accused of favoring white men for the top jobs. Of course, you vehemently deny the accusation. It's only when you go over all the hiring decisions you have made that you come to the realization that, indeed, you are both racially and gender biased.

Only once you have discovered your hidden biases and assumptions can you consciously choose to avoid acting on the basis of them.

The big take-aways

1. Your assumptions are likely to be wrong.
2. You only know half of your assumptions or biases.
3. Take time to discover hidden assumptions.
4. Check your likely assumptions before each meeting or project.
5. Listen for other people's assumptions.

References

1. Mayer, E. A. et al (2015) "Gut/brain axis and the microbiota," *J. of Clinical Investigation*, 125:3, pp. 926-938.

2. Keijzer, F. et al (2013) "What nervous systems do: early evolution, input–output, and the skin brain thesis," ISAB, 21:2 pp. 67-85.

3. McCraty, R. et al (2009) "The Coherent Heart Heart–Brain Interactions, Psychophysiological Coherence, and the Emergence of System-Wide Order," *Integral Review*, 5:2, pp. 1-114.

4. Rilling, J. et al (2008) "The neurobiology of social decision-making," *Current Opinion in Neurobiology*, 18:2, pp. 159-165.

5. Murphy, Gillian et al (2019) "False Memories for Fake News During Ireland's Abortion Referendum," *Psychological Science*, January, 2019.

6. Walker, K. L. (2010) "Do You Ever Listen? Discovering the Theoretical Underpinnings of Empathic Listening," *International Journal of Listening*, 11:1, pp. 127-137.

7. The Big Three are Bain & Co, McKinsey, and Boston Consulting Group.

Chapter 5:
Strategy and the basic human drivers

Humans are driven by four very powerful neurogenetic forces. We call them the CATS. As we're consultants, this must be an acronym, which it is. A strategy that does not fulfil the CATS needs of your customer, clients, or other stakeholders in either its planning or its implementation, is doomed to failure.

On the other hand, if the strategy does give the right people CATS satisfaction, it will almost certainly be a success in meeting its goals.

So, what are CATS? The acronym stands for:

- Certainty;
- Autonomy;
- Trust; and
- Status.

These should be the basis of all your pre-strategy research. Since we are relationship animals first and foremost, CATS are all tied to our need for supportive relationships. They are also about safety, largely relationship safety. You'll see what we mean by this as we examine the workings of each of these drivers.

The need for certainty
In many ways the need for certainty is the most powerful of the CATS. Many people stay in jobs, relationships, even locations long after these have ceased to add value to our lives. We look for predictability, so we know how to respond. Many of us value relational certainty over life itself. An extreme example of this is the motivation of suicide bombers. Studies of failed or would-be suicide bombers have shown that what drives them to suicide is the value they place on the good esteem of their comrades or their leaders. They feel that their sacrifice will give them certainty in that good esteem.

Like all the CATS, we have varying needs for certainty depending on our genetics (for example, our inherited risk tolerance) and our experience.

Of course, all of us seek some certainty in all areas of our lives but, in today's world, certainty is a diminishing commodity. The social and business climate and even the climate itself all seem to be in flux.

However, the general rule is that each of us needs certainty in those areas we care most about. And we are willing to pay a lot or make a considerable sacrifice to achieve it. While nearly all strategic initiatives aim to achieve certainty in one way or another, few succeed because the strategists have failed to look beyond their assumptions as to what other people need in this regard.

There are many examples where people's need for certainty was misjudged. For example, take Iridium.

Iridium was a company that produced global satellite phones – predominantly for the yachting market, for sailors who needed communication outside of the range of traditional radio. Backed by Motorola, it spent $5 billion to expand and launch its wireless satellite phone range. To work, the system relied on 66 satellites, which were not yet in place. In an effort to make this happen, the company put itself in $1.5 billion of debt.

Further, each handset was priced at $3,000 and cost $5 a minute per call, on top of other significant monthly charges. Customers rejected this and in 1999 the company filed for bankruptcy, less than a year after launching.

The company's strategy relied on the assumption that the user's need for certainty of communication in any situation would trump the high cost of obtaining it. As it turned out this assumption was wrong – as most are – and so the company failed.

What should they have done? First, as we have seen, not rely on their assumptions about how much their customers would pay for this particular certainty. Second, ask if their potential customers really valued certainty in this area. Finally, find out what other options customers might have.

Most of the clients for the service would have been people who owned yachts and who sailed beyond the reach of standard radio communication. In fact, the number of these yachties is relatively small, and also mostly not super-rich. Many are drawn to long-distance sailing for the thrill of being out of touch. Certainty of communication might not be very important to them and certainly not worth spending about $5,500 in today's money for the handset and $9 per minute to make a call.

The real questions to be asked are:

- In what area do these yachties need certainty?
- What would they be prepared to pay for certainty in this area?
- How can my technology match their capacity to pay?
- What other options do they have that might meet their needs?
- Can my technology meet another CATS need – status, or autonomy, for example?

The drive for autonomy defeats the best strategies

Autonomy is another very powerful CATS need. It is the ability to have control over your work and life. Most of the work/life balance discussions that we read and hear about are really around the need for autonomy.

If, through your strategic initiative, you can give your clients, customers, or employees a sense that your product, service, or leadership can increase their sense of control over their life or circumstances, then your strategy is far more likely to succeed.

Bear in mind that those who have a high need for certainty might not have the same drive for autonomy. In fact, many people find safety, or relational support, in having a low level of autonomy. Look at people who stay in controlling relationships even when they involve abuse. Or those who prefer jobs where they have little input in exchange for job security. Others have a very high need for autonomy and when that need is frustrated, they can become very angry, anxious, or even suffer a breakdown.[1]

Much has been written about the failure of Blackberry. It had a great start and was favored by managements because it had fewer distracting features – especially games – than the iPhone or Androids, and superior security. Blackberry's strategy was to provide the kind of smartphone that company managements wanted. In the beginning, when it had very limited competition, this strategy worked.

The problem was that, although sales to managements continued to climb, the usage of their phones went down. Employees complained, essentially, about the loss of autonomy to use smartphones in ways that suited them. To them, their sense of being in control of an important part of their lives was telling. In the end the tech departments of corporations and professional service companies yielded to the demands of the end users of the equipment and Blackberry collapsed. Near the end it changed its technology to be more like an Android but by then it was too late.

Blackberry could have saved itself by realizing earlier that the lack of autonomy that its device offered was a killer. A new strategy was needed and the first thing that those who devised it should have asked is "How can our smartphone add to the autonomy – the sense that using our smartphones will give them added control over their lives – of our end users?" Both Apple and Samsung were smart enough to spend a lot of time researching the answer and the result was that they destroyed Blackberry.

Blackberry's sales strategy was to concentrate its pitch firmly in the B2B space, without realizing that in reality they were in the B2C area because the ultimate users would call the shots. It was the users' autonomy that counted.

Nobody trusts your strategy

The third element in CATS is trust. All strategic initiatives come down to trust. The less trust in management, the less likely a company is to successfully implement its strategy. Some studies have shown that, worldwide, only 13 percent of employees are engaged at work.[2] The main reason for this lack of engagement is lack of trust in managers, which overall is very low. Research shows that over 60 percent of employees don't trust their bosses.[3]

Our own surveys show an even higher level of distrust.[4] Trust between colleagues at the same level is fairly high, at 60 to 80 percent, but this is declining with the increasing reliance on technology and the consequent fear of job loss. One recent survey showed only 20 to 30 percent having a high level of trust in colleagues.[5] Trust in immediate supervisors or managers is around 40 to 60 percent. Trust in senior management bumps around the 30 to 40 percent level.

In line with this is the worldwide decline in trust in brands. Professor Klaus Schwab, founder and chairman of the World Economic Forum, explains that "There are four prerequisites of a company's survival: profitability, growth, risk protection, and earning public trust".[6] While we may expect people to sometimes lie, like athletes, actors, and most certainly politicians, we don't expect brands to lie. Why would global companies risk their brand equity by outright lying to their customers?

Most certainly this is done to increase profits and because customers know this, they no longer trust what advertisers or company executives say.

Take the case of Volkswagen. Volkswagen was, until recently, the world's largest car maker and one of the most trusted auto brands. Its management lied about its emissions tests through using software its engineers developed for the purpose. Why would a mega brand risk its reputation? Profit seems to have been the goal. Jointly, German car manufacturers actively promoted to Americans the idea that diesel was the future, a way to meet tougher US emission standards. The only way VW was able to compete and live up to the promise was to lie. Its arrogance in thinking it wouldn't get caught is interesting, especially since it publicly promised to be the "greenest" car producer in the world by 2018. VW claimed its diesel engine was superior – selling over 12.6 million of them. The fact that buyers paid a $2,700 premium over gasoline engines for VW diesels meant an additional $34 billion in VW's bank account. But the real problem was that its engines emitted nitrogen oxide pollutants up to 40 times above US standards – environmental damage that can't be fixed. VW faced what is called a "trust tax" or the cost to a brand of losing public trust.

In a CNN Money report, Credit Suisse estimated the cost of the VW diesel emissions scandal could exceed $86 billion. About the same GDP value as a country like Ecuador. Volkswagen is facing a very big trust tax.

Its strategy – lying to the regulators and the public about emissions from its diesel engines in order to sell more cars – failed, possibly terminally for the company. Humans have a need to trust and be trusted. Our natural instinct is to trust, but once that is lost it's almost impossible to regain it.

Indeed, the need to trust is part of our DNA and, with the other CATS, one of the most important factors in human life. The findings from numerous studies into human biology show that the need to trust and be trusted is associated with specific hormones, in particular oxytocin, as well as specific brain structures, which are located in the basal ganglia, limbic system, and the frontal cortex.[7]

We'll be looking at the how-to of gaining trust in Chapter 11, but for now it's sufficient to say that mutual trust is vital for a strategy to succeed.

Status hunger gets in the way

Status for all mammals – including humans – is about safety. We don't usually think of it that way; we think of status as having to do with position, belongings, and so forth. But our DNA formed at a time when our species didn't have leaders as such, and we didn't have personal possessions. Status came with usefulness to the band or the tribe.

Think of a troop of baboons on the African savannah. In times of danger – say the approach of a lion or leopard – they all scamper up trees. According to game wardens we spoke to, the baboons with the highest status in the troop are allowed to go to the top of the tree, while the lowest status animals take their place on the lowest branches. If the predator climbs the tree, the lowest status individuals get eaten.

Almost every primate species, including ourselves, protects those of their group who are perceived to be the most valuable, the ones most able to protect or nourish the tribe. Status is therefore linked to social utility and support, but also to safety, since high-status animals will be protected and favored (except by their rivals for status).

In humans the desire for safety is the prime driver for an individual to provide social value. We only feel really safe when people value us, when they rely on us, when they give us a sense of status.

A good strategy therefore should give its stakeholders a sense of status – a sense that we value them for their contribution to our welfare. This is true of both the end users – the customers – and those tasked with implementing the strategy. If the only ones who get a status benefit from a policy are those who originated it – for example, the CEOs of the firms in a merger – then it is almost bound to fail.

Another reason for failure is that the leader of the business sees success or failure in terms of their own perceived status through material reward. This is true in Donald Trump's numerous business failures (think Trump Airlines, Trump Vodka, Trump Mortgages, Trump Casinos, Trump Towers (hotels), Trump University and Trump: The Game – a board game) and, if possible, even more so in the case of Jeffrey Skilling and the collapse of Enron. In both cases their strategy was simply to feed their monumental narcissism.

The big take-aways

1. Make sure you feed everyone's CATS.
2. Not everyone has the same CATS needs so take the time to discover what your stakeholders' real CATS needs are.
3. Ask yourself "Whose status am I aiming to elevate?" with your strategy. If it is just yours, drop it.

References

1. Vansteenkiste, M. and Ryan, R. M. (2013) "On psychological growth and vulnerability: Basic psychological need satisfaction and need frustration as a unifying principle." *Journal of Psychotherapy Integration*, 23:3, pp. 263-280.

2. Beck, R. and Harter, J. (2015) "Managers Account for 70% of Variance in Employee Engagement," *Gallup Business Journal*, 21 April 2015.

3. Bylok, F., Tomski, P., Jelonek, D. and Wyslocka, E. (2017) Managing organizational trust – orientation towards trust in an enterprise." *Paper presented at the Second International Conference on Economic and Business Management.*

4. Fortinberry, A. and Murray, B. (2018) *Leading the Future; The Human Science of Law Firm Leadership and Strategy.* ARK Group, London, UK.

5. Bylok, F. et al, 2017.

6. Quoted in Rozdeba, D. (2016) "Lies and the declining trust in brands," *Branding Strategy Insider*, 4 January 2016.

7. Riedl, R. and Javor, A. (2012) "The biology of trust: Integrating evidence from genetics, endocrinology, and functional brain imaging." *Journal of Neuroscience, Psychology, and Economics*, 5:2, pp. 63-91.

Chapter 6:
Humanizing strategy

Most corporate strategies are written so that they have very little to do with human beings, and you often wonder what on earth the folks who worked day and night on them were thinking about.

One thing we know is that their minds are taken up with things like the organization's financial performance, market opportunities, competitive advantage, and operating model. There's usually nothing there of the remotest interest to a human being.

We talked to David Brown, the group CEO of Solgen Energy Group, one of the leaders in the solar energy business, about how he sees strategy.

"Look," he said. "Strategy is like a lot of words corporate types use – 'differentiation' and so forth. It's a word which in reality describes nothing meaningful about the company, and by that, I mean the people, the team, the tribe. It describes nothing real. Success comes from being 'real'. Differentiation is about having the best team, the most responsive people. It's being there for customers. It's listening to them. Our strategy is how we do things, how we go about things. My 'strategy' is to make my team happy because then they'll be innovative and give the customer the best service. Strategy must be about people."

What is a "human" strategy?

When we spoke to Tristram Carfrae, deputy chairman of Arup, the multinational firm of engineers, designers, and architects employing 16,000 people around the world, he made a similar point to Brown:

> "People have to see that strategy works for them. It's got to be about 'being human'. There have to be enough of their voices at the table when the strategy is drawn up."

Mark Rigotti (the managing partner of Herbert Smith Freehills whom we quoted earlier), Brown, and Carfrae all see the process of strategy formulation somewhat differently. To Rigotti it's something that's constantly open to change, more a tactical response to a changing market. To Brown it's essentially a way of engaging the workforce. To Carfrae it's a slower and more deliberative process, a shift in culture rather than business economics.

But they all agree about the "humanness" of it. What does this mean? What they agree on is that the formulation of strategy is not a top-down model. It's not just the Board, the C-suite, and their advisors who arrive at the strategic plan and then hand it down as if in stone from the mount. They all agree that a strategy formulated in that way is doomed to failure.

The most successful strategists in Bob's experience were the hunter-gatherers that he lived with for a year on the plains of southern Africa. They had a simple way of coming to a strategic decision. First the council of elders (essentially everyone over the age of about 40 in the band of 53 people) determined that an important decision had to be made – for example, a move to a new hunting ground. They would then call a meeting of everyone over the age of six.

At this meeting, everyone was encouraged to participate. The final decision was only taken when all of those present agreed on the course of action. Sometimes these meetings would go on for days. The important thing is that everyone in the band felt listened to and everyone had a stake in the outcome.

Bob witnessed many heated disputes in these meetings and often lots of shouting. Sometimes it seemed like the men enjoyed shouting over each other. But in the end a decision was always reached. The decisions were nearly always right, in that they were enacted by everyone and enabled the band to thrive – a much higher rate of success than corporate strategies.[1]

Steps towards humanizing a strategy

Of course, in a firm the size and structure of Arup it may not be practical to get everyone's buy-in on all major decisions, although it does work if the culture of the business or even the country supports that level of consensus.[2]

Our neurogenetics evolved to cope with the challenges of being in a relatively small group – almost no hunter-gatherer bands had over 100 people in them, the more usual size was between ten and 50.

However, the hunter-gatherer model can guide us towards a way of coming to a strategic decision that will be accepted and supported by nearly all the employees of an enterprise.

First, there must be a council of elders (CE) equivalent. This shouldn't just be the Board and/or the C-suite (although it usually is, which is a pity) but should be a broader representation of the organization as a tribe. It need not be large; indeed, a CE over seven to ten people is already unwieldy and inherently low performing. Their job is to decide if change is needed, and then work out the reason for a new strategy or change. Because this CE is broadly representative, there is more chance that the reasoning behind the need for change will be accepted by the bulk of employees.

The CE's job is then to take that reasoning to focus groups and put the case for change. Only when there's broad consensus about the need for a new strategy is it possible to move forward.

The actual strategy and the ways in which it will be implemented should be decided by the CE and the C-suite/Board. That then goes back to the focus groups for comment and any ideas for changes or alterations – after all, it's the employees in general who will decide whether the implementation is a success or failure.

Of course, in a smaller company the CE and the focus groups may not be needed because management – assuming it's trusted by the employees – can negotiate directly with them.

That itself is an issue. Over 80 percent of managers believe they are trusted by their employees, yet up to 70 percent of employees don't trust their management. If the trust isn't there, as we've said earlier, no strategy can succeed because the resistance to any change will be too great.

Meeting people's real needs

A strategy, as Carfrae says, is "essentially the basis for a number of relationships". Any relationship is a mutual satisfaction of need. If I have a need that you can meet, and you have a need that I can meet, then we will form a relationship if only to get those needs met. The more needs we can mutually satisfy, the stronger the relationship will be.

Recent research has shown that an employee who feels that his or her needs are not being met will not be happy and will in fact be in danger of suffering from mental ill health – especially depression and anxiety.[3] What's more, without the sense that their needs are being taken as important, employees' performance deteriorates and their openness to change will be much lower than otherwise.[4]

So, what are the needs that must be met? In 1943 Abraham Maslow formulated his now well-known "hierarchy of needs".[5] He cited the basic needs as air, food, water, warmth, shelter, rest and sex. We would agree with those of course, since without these, life cannot last long or be passed on.

As a second tier, Maslow cited "love and belonging," "esteem," and "self-actualization".[6] At the time Maslow was writing it was not understood how all these needs were tied together and how strong the need for relationships was.

More recent research, and our own observation, shows that it is not uncommon for people to value relationships more than life itself – witness soldiers sacrificing their lives for their comrades and loved ones at home. Interrogations of unsuccessful suicide bombers reveal that their real motivation is not so much ideology but the esteem of their handlers and loyalty to the group. Indeed, in later decades Maslow modified his hierarchy and took out much of the rigidity of the classification.[7]

These relationship-focused needs are the ones that matter as far as the stakeholders in any strategy initiative are concerned. The purpose of strategy from the point of view of those who work for the organization is to secure the future of the tribe and to give those within it a sense of safety and purpose.

These four universal needs, as we see them, are for:

- Physical safety. As we have said, to human beings the prime universal element in physical safety is to be surrounded with a network of supportive relationships;

- Emotional security. In any relationship we need to know that we are relationally safe – that the other person values us. We are constantly on the lookout for any changes in the way that the other person behaves towards us. We need constancy in our relationships;

- Attention. Because of how adult attachment works we are always seeking attention – particularly from parent figures such as clients or work superiors; and

- Importance. We discussed this in the context of the need for status, one of the four CATS drivers. We need to feel important to those we depend on in order to feel safe.

All the above needs are about safety, since as we have seen, all our relationships are based on that need. We'd like to look at each of these needs in relation to strategy and change.

Physical safety

The walls of a castle, or the locks on a house door, may make you feel safe. However, since our genetics were formed before we had such things, they are a substitute for the intrinsic need to be together with people who "have your back". Physical safety also includes, fairly obviously, a living wage – whatever that means to a particular person – as well as being able to keep one's job and, equally obviously, a safe place to work.

The people you work with are one of your tribes, perhaps your most important one in our present society, since many people spend most of their waking hours working. To a hunter-gatherer, exclusion from the band meant almost certain death. The stress of cumulative job-loss has been shown to cause heart attacks, even decades later.[8] In men this shock can be passed via their sperm to their offspring and cause the next generation to suffer from cardiac and other health problems.

Job insecurity is one of the primary reasons that strategic implementations fail.[9] If people are afraid of losing their job, they probably won't care enough to make implementation a success.

Before embarking on the implementation of a strategy it's imperative to make sure, as much as possible, that the key people charged with carrying out the new policy feel that their own jobs are safe, and the same is true of those they work with. People need to feel that their "tribe" will stay together.

Exquisite Soft Toys was a British toy manufacturer. A mid-sized company, it was nevertheless one of the largest producers of soft cuddly teddy bears and the like in Europe. At the time Bob was advising a rival firm, also based in the UK.

Both Bob and the MD of Exquisite faced the same problem – similar but cheaper Asian-made toys were flooding the market. Although the quality was not comparable to the British product, Bob realized that in time it would be. Also, children were becoming more interested in electronic and digital toys than the traditional soft toy.

Bob and his rival decided on different strategies. Exquisite opted to stay in essentially the same business but to go up-market and appeal more to adults. Bob realized that the skills his firm's employees had and the factory the firm leased could both be used in an entirely different industry – the ink-jet printing of large images that could be used in theatres, interior decorating, advertising and so on.

Since Exquisite's new strategy required far fewer machines and people to work them, the company had to radically downsize. The implementation of its new plan was stymied by poor quality control, the loss of key workers, presenteeism and low morale, probably the result of job insecurity. Exquisite went out of business shortly after.

The company Bob helped reinvent itself was very profitable and eventually sold to a Japanese conglomerate. All of the workers kept their jobs and worked enthusiastically to implement the changes.

Emotional security

Emotional security is essentially about relationships and, in particular, adult attachment in the working environment. Adult attachment is similar to attachment between carers and children. A child's desire to be close to its parents is very similar to an adult's desire to be close to the object of their attachment, be it a romantic partner or a supportive supervisor or a work colleague.

We spoke about how fear of job loss leads employees to reject corporate strategy. This fear is not just of reduced income; it is also the emotional pain of losing those you're attached to.

While many people believe that work relationships are somehow less intense, or at least different from, other relationships, the truth is that the brain does not make these distinctions. Loss of a close colleague can be not only difficult but traumatic.

The impact can be even greater for those who had poor attachment as a child. Colleagues, particularly senior colleagues and managers who were supportive of you may become quasi-parental figures who gave you what your parents couldn't – a sense that you belonged and that you were protected.

To make a strategy successful – especially in its implementation – management must understand that fear and allow for it in planning the initiative.

For example, management of a large law firm in Atlanta decided on what to them was a matter of simple administrative convenience. They wanted to save space and rent by eliminating a floor. To do this they had to move a majority of their legal and non-legal staff to different floors, which involved splitting intact teams. On the surface all went well. But almost immediately they found that lawyer and non-lawyer productivity and engagement went down by about 25 percent and stayed there for many months.

As a result of a series of interviews and a written survey, we found that this was clearly the result of people feeling separated from those they were attached to.

"What we gained in rent reduction we more than lost in output, engagement and, surprisingly, client satisfaction," the firm's COO told us. "Some of our best people left. Clients were confused by the change and, I believe, put off by the downbeat mood of the partners and lawyers generally."

If this can happen with a simple floor change, think what can happen with a more fundamental strategic initiative!

Attention and importance

Humans have needs around attention and a sense of importance. A child's need for attention is not about attention-seeking, as if it were some sort of pathology. Attention is a fundamental human desire tied in with safety. Children feel safe if people are paying attention to them. In his or her mind it means they aren't going to be abandoned.

Adults are no different. We generally feel safer if we are receiving attention. We feel important, we feel valued and, like children, we feel less likely to be dismissed, laid off, or otherwise abandoned. Of course, adults, like children, can take these needs to extremes.

At work, attention may look like someone stopping in the corridor to chat, or a colleague offering to pick up a cup of coffee for you along with their own. It can mean a boss taking the time to ask how things are going, or to discuss your career. These may seem like small events, but cumulatively they have a big impact. And their absence can have an even bigger effect.

If a strategy looks to the employee as if he or she will lose importance, status, or attention by the initiative then they will, consciously or unconsciously, work against it.

Making needs concrete, timely, and doable

Management must recognize that these needs – physical safety, emotional security, attention, and importance – are natural to all of us and no strategy is going to work out as planned if they are not catered to.

However, one of the problems for executives and strategists – and indeed anyone else – is that most people either don't say what they really want or need or they don't say so in terms that can be met. Usually they use generalities that can't be clearly understood or actioned.

A medium-sized company in northern England (now in Holland) was a maker of craft beer. A decade ago it had started as a four-person operation. Local beer-drinkers took to the product and spread the word. Five years ago a major European supermarket chain began to carry the product and the company's sales soared. By 2016 it was employing nearly 100 people.

The company exported nearly half of its beer to the continent – mostly to Holland, Belgium, and northern France. In fact, its 2015 exports had risen by 35 percent.

When the 2016 Brexit referendum happened, the company's MD, Tom Midfield, realized he had to make a strategic choice. Either he stayed in the UK and faced possible tariffs on his exports to the EU –thereby putting a huge dent in his export sales – or he relocated to Holland (his largest export market) and became a European firm.

Much depended on the reaction of his four key personnel to the possible move – the quality and distinctiveness of his beer depended on them.

As it turned out they all, bar one, thought there was really no option but to move the company to Europe since the UK was a stagnant market – too much competition and a fierce price war – and the EU was a growing one.

We moderated a meeting between Tom and these employees, during which they exchanged needs. We encouraged them to specify their needs under the four headings (physical safety, emotional security, attention and importance) and to use this procedure to negotiate a way forward.

One of the key people's needs under physical safety was: "I need you to provide me with a house in Holland."

As it stood it seemed to be a need that Tom couldn't meet. Alicia then asked the brewer: "What does 'provide a house' mean?"

"Well," he said. I'll need help with buying a new house."

"What kind of help?'

"Help with the deposit."

"What does 'help' mean?"

"A loan to cover the deposit."

So, it turns out that the seemingly impossible becomes very doable.

How needs are expressed is very important. Needs should be concrete, about action not thoughts, beliefs, or emotions, and timely. It should be clear what action is required, when the action is needed, and that it is doable by someone in that position.

Each of the key workers and Tom exchanged needs in this way. As with many clients, the process of concretizing their needs of each other forced them to think not just about what they really required in physical terms, but what was really important to them in terms of their relationships.

The upshot was that the move to Holland was successful and the company is thriving in its new location. Taking the time to think and clearly describe to each other what they needed, and often negotiating these needs in order to reach agreement, put their relationships on a firmer footing. In fact, the company regularly holds "needs-based dialogue" to maintain and build strong connections.

The big take-aways

1. Make sure you have "humanness" at the center of your strategic thought.
2. Seek to find out what your stakeholders' real needs are.
3. Make sure you put people's physical safety, emotional security, attention, and importance as the prime reason for your strategy (of course you also have to make money!).

References

1. Note: Bob lived with a band of hunter-gatherers in Africa for a year as part of his PhD.
2. Lämsä ,T. (2010) "Leadership Styles and Decision-making in Finnish and Swedish Organizations," *Revista de Management Comparat International*, 11:1, pp. 139-149.
3. Slemp, G. R. and Vella-Brodrick, D. A. (2014) "Optimising Employee Mental Health: The Relationship Between Intrinsic Need Satisfaction, Job Crafting, and Employee Well-Being," *Journal of Happiness Studies*, 15:4, pp. 957-977.
4. Judge, T. A. et al (2001) "The job satisfaction–job performance relationship: A qualitative and quantitative review," *Psychological Bulletin*, 127:3, pp. 376-407.
5. Maslow, A. H. (1943). "A Theory of Human Motivation," *Psychological Review*, 50:4, pp. 370-96.
6. Maslow, A. H. (1987) Motivation and personality (3rd ed.). Delhi, India: Pearson Education, p. 84.
7. Maslow, A. H. (1971) *The farther reaches of human nature*. New York: The Viking Press.
8. Dupre, M. E. et al (2012) "The Cumulative Effect of Unemployment on Risks for Acute Myocardial Infarction," *Archives of Internal Medicine*, 172:22, pp. 1731-1737.
9. Nayak A. C. et al (2016) "Human Capital Engagement – A Key Factor in Merger and Acquisitions," *Splint International Journal of Professionals*, 3:1 pp. 130-136.

Chapter 7:
The culture problem

At some stage, every business we have ever been asked to work for wants us to help them with "culture change" in some form or other. They rarely call what they are looking for by that name and, anyway, there is a lot of confusion around what "culture" actually means.

In essence, culture is merely a means of making sure that members of a group, tribe, society, or business are able to collaborate together, and provide safety for the group.[1] In mass societies such as the ones we live in, or in a medium-to-large size business, there will often be multiple cultures.

However, unless the various cultures are aligned with each other – and have enough in common – the society or the corporation will find it difficult if not impossible to change. A culture has five essential elements. These are:

1. A shared language – which in a corporation can mean a shared use of jargon;

2. Symbols – anything used to represent, express, and stand for an event, situation, or idea. They are used to guide behavior. For example, wearing a hard hat (or not) on a building site is a cultural symbol as much as a cross is in a predominantly Christian culture. They both direct us to actions that make us part of the tribe;

3. Norms – both the unwritten rules of the society and "the way things are done around here";

4. Values – often the way in which we differentiate ourselves as a group. Values define what is "good" or "ethical" to the members of the society. Values differ widely from culture to culture; and

5. Beliefs and assumptions – our joint beliefs and assumptions are our refuge, regardless of whether they are religious beliefs or merely the assumptions we all share about the world.

Each of these elements are equally important. Culture change or strategic implementation involves reconciling the differences between how individuals or subgroups view them. That's essentially what cultural alignment means. Lack of cultural alignment is why so many strategies fail.

The "why" of culture

As we said, culture is both the "why" and the "how" of cooperation. Those who do not share the elements that make up a culture will generally not easily collaborate.

This is vital when considering any strategic initiative. Your people work for and with you because by doing so they can join your culture or one or other of the cultures that exist in a larger firm. Although people form cultures to enable collaboration, this is not their conscious motive.

The principal cognitive driver of culture is safety. Being a member of a group that shares common ideas, assumptions, rules, and rituals gives you a feeling of belonging and of being protected.

Often a new strategy will be seen as a threat to the culture and therefore a danger to the members' sense of safety. It is liable to be fiercely resisted. Management then turns to us or to other consultants, hoping that the miracle of "culture change" will enable the new direction to be accepted.

Some strategies require adjustments, or even wholesale change, to the culture in order to succeed. New ways of working such as agile are a case in point. If the culture has been hierarchical, competitive and rule-bound, much work will be needed to build the trust, mutual support, and courage to try new things that enable this highly flexible approach.

But trying to make a new culture is not possible without knowing how the human system works.

Why are there competing cultures?

There have always been, and always will be, competing cultures. Humans are only capable of making about 100-150 close relationships (close here means "mutually supportive"). It's the famous "Dunbar Number" postulated by Professor Robin Dunbar, head of the Social and Evolutionary Neuroscience Research Group in the Department of Experimental Psychology at the University of Oxford.[2]

Since culture is about cooperation and safety, it follows that the maximum size of a homogenous culture is about 150 individuals. This is the same size as the largest hunter-gatherer band. Beyond that the group will split, with some members going off to form their own cultural group. This is why, in evolutionary terms, we have various "splitting personality disorders". They served a useful purpose 10,000 years ago since a human band larger than about 100 or so would be too big for a particular foraging area.[3]

Why strategy and culture must fit together

From all this it's obvious that any strategy must fit in with the culture of those who have to implement it, and with those (including customers or clients) who will be affected by it.

Not long ago we were working with two large media companies that were trying to merge. The managements of both companies could see a clear financial reason for merging, as there would be vast synergies and cost savings in the proposed merger.

The problem was that they both had a number of totally different cultures. For example, one of the outfits concentrated on producing films and TV programs, while the other was much more into distribution and owned a cable network and a cinema chain. The overall culture in the programming company was relaxed, creative, and flat in terms of management structure.

The distribution company had a top-down management configuration and was bureaucratic and very siloed. Each silo had its own cultural variation on the central theme.

We advised them that the merger wouldn't work, that there was insufficient alignment between the cultures of the two operations, and, what's more, the number of competing cultures in the distribution company would make it very difficult for the firm to execute any major change.

They went ahead anyway; a large amount of money was spent, and after two years the two operations demerged. The culture clashes within and between the two divisions made it impossible for the promised synergies and cost savings to materialize. They simply were unable to work together.

Change the culture or change the strategy?

The merger above presented the management of both companies with a dilemma – the merger strategy and the cultures of the firms were incompatible. Although it wasn't realized at the time, one had to go.

Management opted to try to change the culture. They set down a series of behavioral rules and instituted a clutch of "values" that they expected every employee in the merged enterprise to adopt. Fairly soon after they did this the various cultures did unite around one thing – a hatred and a distrust of the new joint management.

Prior to the merger we surveyed the level of trust in the separate companies and we repeated the exercise about six months after the merger. We found that the level of trust in management had gone down by over 35 percent throughout the organization.

By the time the C-suite and the Board of the combined business got around to deciding that they had to do something about culture, it was already far too late. The enterprise was doomed. The strategy had failed.

If they had taken a different path, then perhaps all would've been well. There are three steps to make this sort of merger strategy work in terms of overcoming cultural obstacles:

1. As you set your strategy, ask yourself the simple question: What's in it for those who have to apply it and work within it? If the only reason behind the plan is to make or save more money for the executives or shareholders, go back to square one and come up with a new one.

2. Ask yourself another question: what kind of corporate culture would be needed for the plan to succeed? How closely aligned is this with the existing culture(s) within the businesses you wish to merge?

3. Work out a plan for cultural alignment.

This is exactly what David Brown did when he was hired by the Australian conglomerate Wesfarmers to merge three quite different insurance companies into one – Wesfarmers Insurance.

The how-to of culture change

The three entities were spread over the continent (Victoria (with a branch in New South Wales), and Western Australia). All had completely different customer bases and maybe because of this they had very different cultures. Two of them (the ones based in WA) sold directly to the public. One company sold directly to agricultural enterprises and farmers and the other marketed general insurance and was based in Perth. Both were relatively small in size.

Since Wesfarmers was Perth-based, it was natural that the general insurance business was the first to be absorbed, shortly followed by the agricultural insurance enterprise. They had completely different products, were in totally different markets, and had completely different cultures. In fact, from the first there were constant fights between the two over resources, funding, and a number of other issues. By the time Brown came on the scene they hardly spoke to each other.

The third entity was on the East Coast and was headquartered in Melbourne with a branch in Sydney. This company was different from the other two in that it sold its products through brokers and had little, if any, dealings with the public. It was also much larger, and far less entrepreneurial.

Shortly after the beginning of the process of amalgamating the three companies we were brought in to help create more unity. It was obvious to us that without a meaningful cultural alignment there was no chance of going forward. We advised and helped implement the cultural aspect of the merger and helped establish a level of trust between the three entities. We were brought in to advise on and help implement the cultural aspect of the merger and to help establish a level of trust between the three entities.

"I had to pick on a number of very simple things that the employees of all three companies could agree on," Brown said after Wesfarmers sold the business for over a billion dollars. The simplest things included a desire for the amalgamated business to thrive so that those who chose to stay on could benefit.

Our team set about doing two things that fit in very well with Brown's demand for simplicity, for what he calls "the basics". Firstly, we set about creating what we call a Behavioral Charter. We got all the employees to agree on a set of very simple values – respect for each other and their clients, trust, and collaboration. There were, of course, many other suggestions, but these three got the largest number of votes from everyone in the three companies.

We then created focus groups to decide what specific behaviors best demonstrated those values. Every generalization is dangerous because there can be disagreement as to what it means and what action is being asked for. For that reason, one of the rules of the exercise was to make the actions concrete. For example, under respect you might have "we say 'thank you' when someone helps us," whereas "we will be polite to each other" would not be specific enough. Under trust, "we will always tell the truth to each other," is acceptable but "supporting each other," is not. Under collaborate they chose "we will share all relevant marketing information with each other", rather than something like "we will cooperate with each other".

We wound up with over 30 actions that all employees voted on and the top ten were chosen for the Charter. These were not the only behavioral norms that developed – far from it – but they were what we call "catalyst behaviors". They encouraged – and in some cases necessitated – other actions that exemplified the values. The process of forming the Charter also influenced people to make agreements based on clear, specific actions that could be observed. This helped avoid misunderstandings and build trust.

The remarkable thing about this document is that almost all the employees at Wesfarmers Insurance adhered to it. Along with leadership and dialogue training that we provided, and a number of policies Brown brought in, the Charter formed the basis of a strong and unified culture.

The Charter behaviors were incorporated into KPIs and informed ratings and decisions about hiring and promotions. Greater clarity of expectations, a core of consistent behaviors, and better dialogue and ways to prevent and negotiate conflict, significantly enhanced alignment and peoples' sense of belonging and safety. Commitment to the business and productivity rose.

"In these values and behavioral norms," Brown said, "they found commonality, and with commonality they found unity."

The big take-aways

1. Work on creating a unified culture before you announce your strategy.
2. Create a Behavioral Charter that all can agree on.
3. Make sure your strategy aligns with the culture.

References

1. Gachter, S. et al (2010) "Culture and cooperation", *Phil. Trans. R. Soc.* B, 365, pp. 2,651-2,661.
2. Dunbar, R. (2010) *How many friends does one person need? Dunbar's number and other evolutionary quirks.* London: Faber and Faber.
3. Stevens, A. and Price, J. (2000) *Evolutionary Psychiatry*, Routledge, London.

Chapter 8:
Leadership for strategy implementation

Since we can never really tell whether any decision is the right one until after the event, we can also never say with any confidence that any strategy will be the right one until 20/20 kicks in.

What we do know for absolute certainty is that an inappropriate leadership style – or the wrong leader – will doom any strategic initiative. According to several Gallup studies, the majority of US corporate leaders are both ineffective generally and bad at leading people in particular.[1] And, as we mentioned before, they are not seen as very trustworthy. This is not a combination that instills confidence.

For example, we have watched with some horror leaders get too involved in the process to the extent that they micromanage everything to do with the implementation of their pet scheme, excluding their most talented people. We have also seen leaders move too fast, creating too much change at once, including ongoing waves of mass redundancies, unnerving those they most want to retain. And we have seen them move too slowly or incrementally, so that the business did not keep up with changing client demands and the business environment.

Even if the strategy is so good that it seems to be 100 percent success guaranteed, these things will kill it.

What is a strategy implementation?
There are generally four ways of implementing a strategy:

1. Direct cutover. Here the new strategy is implemented on day one, usually after some testing (better to test more, but more expensive). It saves a lot of money and is therefore very popular with CFOs. Unfortunately, if it fails (it usually will) the result is a great deal of angst and the failure of the whole operation;

2. Parallel. Both the old and new systems operate side-by-side for a period of time. Both are maintained and kept up to date so that in the event of the failure of the new system, the organization can

fall back on the old one. It is an expensive option and very labor intensive, and there is a danger of staff ignoring (as they usually do) the new system in favor of the old one – as will most managers. Or, in some cases, the new option is seen as sexier and draws to it the most capable staff leading to a failure of the old (and maybe better) one. However, if the system is critical to the running of the organization and any problems would cause enormous difficulties, running operations in parallel is probably the safest option;

3.   Phased. This involves bringing in the new system one step at a time – assuming anyone is capable of doing this successfully and keeping to some sort of timetable; and

4.   Pilot. One section or department in the organization is completely changed over to the new system. Any "bugs" are ironed out before the system is extended to the whole organization.

Any of these can work and which one you choose will depend on the competence of the leadership team. The important thing is that it is best to choose one and try to stick to it. What doesn't work is deciding that one isn't successful for some reason or other and then abruptly changing it. The new one will probably also be unsuccessful and a third one will be initiated. Those tasked with carrying out the strategy will essentially give up and go home. We saw this happen with a major American bank. We were brought in after the fifth attempt at implementing a strategy they called "radical simplification". By this time no one but those of C-suite rank was taking any notice of management directives regarding the strategy. The CEO was eased out shortly after.

The danger of the loss of management interest in the initiative

There's an old cliché that goes, "This, too, shall pass". According to all the usual sources it comes from either medieval Sufi poets or even earlier Jewish ones before it was taken up in the 19th century in the writings of Edward Fitzgerald – you know, "the moving finger" and all that.

Nowadays it refers to what happens to most strategic – or other – initiatives. This, too, will pass, so don't bother about it too much. Much Sturm und Drang from management and their posse of consultants, signifying, in the end, very little.

Another problem is that often management simply seems to lose interest. A couple of years ago we were asked by another bank, this time one of the large Australian ones, to work on changing the culture in their largest and most crucial division. We were astonished by the fact that although the bank was bringing in large structural changes that would affect the working lives of all of them, the leaders of those divisions seemed uninterested.

We asked a number of them why. "We have been through over ten of these 'strategic changes' in the past three years," one of their senior managers said. "None lasts and in the end it all stays the same."

We've seen this loss of focus, if not interest, in insurance companies, banks, law firms, vast multinationals and much, much smaller businesses. In fact, it's the case more often than not. Management loses interest, moves on to other things, and assumes that somehow, someone is picking up the pieces. We've witnessed this even in a five-person business!

Loss of management interest in strategic projects is the norm.[2]

Why should this happen, and with such frequency? The main problem is that most strategic implementations take time, and managers – like all human beings – want to see the results as soon as possible. We are not really long-term creatures; we have short attention spans. We can maintain attention for the long-term, but we vastly prefer not to.

We are also novelty-seeking creatures, even when we're at the top of the management tree. This novelty-seeking trait is built into our neurobiology and is strongly tied in with our reward system.[3] In a sense we are addicted to novelty and it takes a great power of will to drag ourselves into a state of mind where we can maintain interest in almost anything – except another addiction.

Being novelty-addicted worked for us in hunter-gatherer times as it enabled us to cope with changes in the environment – to try new foods, explore new places, forge new tools and so forth.

Aggressive novelty-seeking continues into men's 50s and women's 40s.[4] This is the age of wisdom. After this age people may seek new ideas and ways of thinking, but are not so swayed by the latest fad. Studies at Harvard and elsewhere have shown that no corporate male leader should be below 45 and no female under 35.

How does a leader or a strategist overcome this problem – outside of getting a few years older?

The first thing is to delegate the strategic initiative to someone else, while you stay in charge of the overall business. Then he or she should divide the project into several parts lead by different people.

The person in overall charge of the initiative should ensure they have sufficient variety by collaborating closely with their reports on different aspects of it.

Senior management should only be involved at the beginning and the end of the project or when something seems to be going wrong and the ultimate decision-maker needs to be involved.

The role of leadership

Before we discuss leadership let us get rid of one misconception. It has been trendy to make a sharp distinction between "leadership," defined reasonably well as the ability to influence, motivate and develop people, and "management," which some say is about controlling a group to accomplish a goal. In this book we use the terms managers and leaders interchangeably. Anyone wishing to wield authority or influence only succeeds by engaging others and getting people committed to the relationship with them. The followers' brains then organize themselves to take on board and enact the leader's values and goals in order to strengthen that relationship. Commitment to the organization comes through dedication to the leaders.

The only way to really galvanize people to carry out change is through the strength of their relationship – real or potential – with those who are asking them to do so. This involves engagement with the immediate manager (or in a more matrixed or agile organization, multiple colleagues and managers) through to the CEO, who in large organizations is seen by most employees as a figurehead.

Although much has been written about the numerous management styles on offer, there are, in reality, only three broad types:

- Transactional leadership;
- Laissez-faire leadership; and
- Transformational leadership.

All three have their place in different circumstances and at different times, given that the leader can gain people's confidence and commitment. This is equally true in rolling out strategies or in day-to-day oversight of work. Each style is based on human evolution and therefore on our genetics, and can add value in the right circumstances.

The wrong approach to leadership is to use only one of the three kinds exclusively.

Transactional leadership

Most leaders tend to be largely transactional. This "do it my way" approach fits many corporate bosses because it's simple, and they don't have to discuss, explain, or compromise anything about their commands. "Just do it," the boss cries. It fits in with the authoritarian A-type personality that Boards seem to like.

Transactional leadership was rationalized through a misinterpretation of the works of Charles Darwin in the 1800s. Darwin's idea of "survival of the fittest" was interpreted as "survival of the strongest". CEOs went *mano e mano* against each other. Managers went *mano e mano* against members of their teams. All of them seemingly trying to prove something about their testosterone.

GE is a great case in point. Shortly after taking control of GE, Jack Welch initiated his plan to change the very structure and identity of General Electric – changing it from an electrical manufacturing business to a "service entity". Welch's "services" were to become primarily those accomplished through banking and insurance. He hated manufacturing. This was nothing that Welch kept secret, but readily admitted to.

Welch had a gargantuan task in front of him as General Electric was originated to do two things: to create electricity (generators, power distribution equipment) and to create a demand for usage of their generated electricity within industry and the residential consumer (manufacturing equipment, home heating, appliances, etc.) A virtually perfect set up that worked for over 100 years. Thomas Edison, being one of the founding fathers of the General Electric Company, attests to its origins as an electrical manufacturing and research/development company. Welch was a very authoritarian CEO, with a poor idea of strategy who was unable to listen to anybody's advice but his own. By the time he left, the company had been nearly destroyed by its own internal competition (which he encouraged) and his exclusively transactional style. Darwin would have been horrified.

Human beings operate badly under transactional leaders.[5] The genetic need for consensus decision-making is so much part of our DNA that it is very difficult to shift. We can tolerate a limited amount of "do it now" in times like the Great Depression, the Second World War, or the more recent Great Recession – but by and large it doesn't work for us.

How is it that organizations – and even nations – can come to over-rely on a form of leadership that doesn't work over the long or even medium term? Robert Wright, author of the bestselling book *A Short History of Progress* asserts that our society has proceeded so rapidly that the skills and customs we learned as children are outdated by the time we are 30. In a sense, we struggle to keep up with our own culture.

In hunter-gatherer societies the social structure was, for the most part, fixed and egalitarian. "Leadership was diffuse, a matter of consensus, or something earned by merit or example."[6]

Alicia remembers coming into a tiny village clinging to the mountainside in the far reaches of Afghanistan as part of an anthropology expedition in the late 1960s. Unconsciously echoing the cliché, their guide and interpreter asked, "Who is your leader?" "The leader for what?" came the puzzled reply. "We have someone who can communicate for us all with other villages, is that what you mean?"

In ancient times we looked to transactional leaders in times of crisis – and we still do. If there was no time for consensus because the band was about to be attacked, a flood was coming, or the game had ceased to appear, a respected person (male or female) who had the courage to call out "Do as I say, now!" was followed. In those circumstances, the survival of the band required fast, unified compliance.

For the last 10,000 years, since we stopped living in accordance with our genetics and kingship, dictatorship or authoritarianism has come about as a result of crises real or manufactured. Most recently, Donald Trump and Boris Johnson stoked people's fear of being overrun by migrants; Recep Erdogan of Turkey spread fear that people would lose their religion; Nicolas Maduro shouted that the United States was about to invade Venezuela. There's always an excuse, there's always a crisis. And it's the same in industry. Cometh the crisis, cometh the man (it's usually a man).

Most transactional political leaders ruin their countries, and most transactional CEOs ruin their companies – and frequently make fortunes for themselves in doing so.

It follows that any strategy that relies for its implementation on "do it now" will fail in the long run – or even in the medium term.

However, in periods of enormous dislocation when change needs to happen quickly, our genetics still prompt us to look for direction. Leaders need to show that they have confidence in the strategy and are willing to take a stand.

We have observed organizations in which a transactional leader was needed. In these businesses the leadership was often divided or unsure of the way forward. They reverted to a sort of laissez-faire style, often disguising this as empowering downwards.

Laissez-faire leadership

Laissez-faire leadership has most in common with our hunter-gatherer past. Bands had an "advisory board," if you like, made up of elders.

Membership was conferred on those who survived to the age of about 45. People relied on elders for support, wisdom and guidance, but they were not leaders, but more like mentors. Hunter-gather hunting and foraging groups have been said to have been the most highly performing teams (HPTs) in history and it is with HPTs that laissez-faire works best.[7]

HPTs are defined as teams that consistently meet or exceed the goals set for them by the organization. They are made up of capable people who get on well together and are motivated to perform at their best in order to keep the team together. They are small, usually five to seven people. And they are rare – only about five percent of teams meet these criteria. High Performing Teams call for a hands-off approach, in which the leader is available if difficulties arise but mainly runs interference from, and coordinates at high levels with, the rest of the organization.

Some of the new ways of working, including Agile, deploy a more non-hierarchical approach, which in theory fits in with our genetics. However, Agile requires small units (called squads or scrums) that perform highly and whose members enjoy working collegially together, able to support and challenge each other. It requires a high level of goal clarity and accountability. So far, few organizations have been able to make this work. Many are reverting to more traditional leadership structures. All too often, we are seeing leaders consciously or unconsciously use what's really laissez faire leadership as a cover for not understanding or being able to master Agile.

Whatever style you use, remember that the object of the exercise is, as an article in the *Ivey Business Journal* put it, "the survival of the most fitted".[8] This means the most fitted style to the context and the circumstance.

Transformational leadership and the genetics of strategy

The leadership style most suited to the genetics and neurobiology of human beings is what is known as transformational leadership. It is also by far the best for strategic implementation. Unsurprisingly, it is also more often practiced by women (proportionally they have less testosterone and are better at consultation and consensus). However, the best transformational leader to come out of the US was a man – the late great Lee Iacocca, the leader who took over and rescued Chrysler in the 1980s. This style of leadership focuses on coaching and developing people. It calls on the kind of dialogue skills we will be discussing in the next chapter, on communicating strategy, to engage and inspire people and gain their commitment.

According to the principal thinker of transformational leadership, Bernard Bass, transformational leadership is about:

- Holding positive expectations for followers, believing that they can do their best;
- Inspiring, empowering, and stimulating followers to exceed normal levels of performance;
- Being skilled at leading and working with complex work groups and organizations and facilitating change;
- Role modeling the behaviors that they desire;
- Being able to guide their followers through an uncertain environment;
- Insisting on the highest standards from their teams, thus challenging and empowering them; and
- Being able to get the greatest loyalty from their people.[9]

In terms of strategy, transformational leaders bring people along rather than use coercion. This is very much in line with the genetics of leadership. The transformational leader becomes rather like a one-person council of elders in a hunter-gatherer band. People invest in the new direction through their commitment to the leader.

The big take-aways

1. Train all your managers in a coaching, transformational leadership style.
2. Give yourself plenty of time to select the right people to lead the implementation.
3. Do not begin any change initiative unless you already have high performing, mutually supportive teams in place to carry it out.

References

1. Harter, J. (2015) "Managers With High Talent Twice as Likely to Be Engaged," *Gallup Economy*, 2 April 2015.
2. Nejati, M. et al (2008) *Issues in Global Business and Management Research: Proceedings of the 2008 International Online Conference on Business and Management (IOCBM 2008)*, Universal Publishers, Irvine, CA.

3. Suhara, S. et al (2001) "Dopamine D2 Receptors in the Insular Cortex and the Personality Trait of Novelty Seeking," *NeuroImage*, 13:5, pp. 891-895.

4. Reio, T. G. and Choi, N. (2004) "Novelty Seeking in Adulthood: Increases Accompany Decline," *The Journal of Genetic Psychology Research and Theory on Human Development*, 165:2, pp. 119-133.

5. Stewart, J. (2006) "Transformational Leadership: An Evolving Concept Examined through the Works of Burns, Bass, Avolio, and Leithwood," *Canadian Journal of Educational Administration and Policy*, Issue #54.

6. Wright, R. (2004) *A Short History of Progress*. House of Anansi Press Toronto, ON.

7. Medinilla Á. (2014) *Team Kaizen*. In: Agile Kaizen. Springer, Berlin.

8. Vandenbosch, M. et al (2019) "Survival of the most fitted", *Ivey Business Journal*, March/April 2019.

9. Bass, B. (1994) *Improving Organizational Effectiveness Through Transformational Leadership*, Sage, NY.

Chapter 9:
The art of communicating strategy

All companies, firms, and government organizations are facing disruption and the strategies that they must forge will therefore be disruptive. What's more, all disruption in these times involves relational disturbance and almost certainly loss. You are going to force some of your employees to cope with the most painful thing that a human being can face – exclusion.[1]

How well you communicate your strategy largely dictates how successful it will be. Mostly it is done badly. Several studies have shown that between just five and eight percent of employees understand any given strategy, and even more alarming, only one in 20 of those charged with implementing the strategy actually implement the strategy that management thinks they're implementing.[2]

There's a communication failure. But the failure is not so much in *what* is communicated but rather *how* it is communicated.

Let us start here with an obvious comment: human beings are designed to communicate face-to-face. But in a large organization that isn't always possible, hence the use of electronic communication of one type or another. In this chapter we'll look at what science and experience say are the best ways to get your strategy across, no matter what communication tools you use.

Remember that how you deliver the message and the emotional impact of the communication is often more important than the facts of the strategy. Knowing this is how Donald Trump won the 2016 presidential election.

In a company or any other organization, large or small, you must be sure that those charged with delivering the message are skilled communicators, which means that they present the message in ways that humans will accept – otherwise you're wasting your time. Marshall McLuhan's famous analogy of the hamburger comes to mind – if the bun and the trimmings don't appeal then you won't sell the burger, no matter how good the meat is.[3]

Communicating strategy is not just telling people what is to happen. It's about getting them so invested in the communicator and the role they play in the implementation of the strategy that they will accept the message no matter how painful.

Strategic listening

As a business leader or manager ask yourself: How well do I know my people? Most corporate or firm leaders are in what Hal Gregersen, executive director of the MIT Leadership Center at Sloan School of Management, calls "a bubble," one that shields them from the reality of what's happening in the world and in their businesses. The higher you rise, the worse it gets.[4]

Giving what may potentially be a hard message involves a number of steps, the first of which must happen long before you start telling people the details of your plan – and ideally before you've any fixed strategy in mind.

This first step is getting to know your people, and the golden rule here is that before you tell you must listen. Humans want and need to be listened to. Unless they feel heard, they will not accept what you have to tell them because they will not think that they are part of the process, or that you have their interests front of mind. They certainly won't make the emotional investment necessary for the strategy, or its implementation, to be successful.

Listen to your clients or customers of course, and to your community. There are many books and articles telling you how to do that, and we don't intend to add to those. We are concerned with how you listen to your internal stakeholders – your employees generally, but especially those who will be asked to implement the strategy.

To really understand your people, you have to engage in "global listening" and the main technique you should use is what we call "mindful listening". Listening is not just about hearing – although that's very important. It's equally about what we call "global listening" – listening in context, listening for understanding, for emotions, and above all for fears and hopes. It's something that a chatbot or an electronic survey can never do. This is a human-to-human, face-to-face exercise.

You're putting what they tell you and the context of what they tell you together to divine their assumptions, beliefs, and biases.

You're trying to understand where they are. This takes time and effort. More than that, it takes "mindful listening" and that has to be taught. Unfortunately, listening training is a very small part of the focus of corporate training and for this reason most leaders and managers, even of Fortune 500 companies, are really bad listeners.[5]

"Mindful listening" is a technique of focusing with intense curiosity on the specific words that people use in relation to everything that you've heard gleaned about the context. Without training, 90 percent of us only really hear about 60 percent of what people say. People's words wash over us without leaving much trace of comprehension. There are several reasons for this:

1. **Reloading**. We tend not to concentrate when people are speaking. Most often we're reloading – thinking about what we're going to say next. When we're doing that, we're unable to hear them in any meaningful way;

2. **Amygdala hijack**. This is a phrase that Daniel Goleman coined in his book *Emotional Intelligence*. What he was referring to was the tendency of the brain to shut down when it feels threatened. The fear center of the brain, the amygdala, takes over all cognitive functions to orchestrate our system for fight, flight, or freeze. The threat can be a sense of personal attack, a feeling of looming danger, or a potential loss of relational support;

3. **Perceptual filter**. We tend to stop listening when what is said challenges our deeply held assumptions or beliefs. Our beliefs and our assumptions, as we said earlier, are very much how we see ourselves, a part of our personality, and we will defend them strongly. Someone attacking or contradicting them is seen to be attacking us at a very profound level. Most of us say we listen with an open mind. In reality, none of us actually do. The reason is that most of our assumptions and beliefs are unconscious – we don't know when we've been triggered; and

4. **We lose interest**. Sometimes we lose interest if our perceptual filter has been activated; other times we lose interest if the conversation isn't relevant to us. A junior lawyer, for example, may be talking to a managing partner (MP) about his concerns over a new strategic initiative that the firm is undertaking, but after a while he sees that the managing partner is no longer really there. The MP has lost interest because what the junior lawyer is saying has little, if any, relevance to the MP.

Being a good listener requires admitting that you probably do some or all of these things. The cure is to make a habit of mindful listening – concentrating on the actual words that people use.

People use certain words for a reason, although usually an uncon-scious one. Often their choice conveys messages they may not aware they are sending. We used to call these "Freudian slips" and believed they were the result of inhibitions around sex. But especially in today's workplace, where we are admonished to separate our personal and work lives and emotions, our preoccupations and concerns slip out. Mindful listening allows you to question the verbal signals about what's really going on with them. Certain words stand out; they shine a torch into the speaker's soul. They're vague, they're emotional, they're personal, sometimes they're out of context. They're telling you something about the speaker without their knowing it. They're inviting you in.

A careless listener lets them go but a mindful listener catches them, asks follow-up questions, or just simply repeats them – inviting the speaker to give you more, to think more deeply, to question their own assumptions.

Asking the right questions

Good asking and good listening go together. Using "global "and "mindful listening" techniques you can discover where the person is emotionally. You know what their hopes, their fears, and their CATS issues are – the main drivers of behavior that we described in chapter five (certainty, autonomy, trust, and status).

But you also need to know where they are cognitively – what their thoughts are. The key here is to combine "mindful listening" with powerful but non-intrusive open-ended questions.

Open-ended questions have unlimited response options. Closed-ended questions are ones that have a limited number of response options – typically "yes" or "no".

For example, an open-ended question might be: "I would be inter-ested to know your thoughts regarding the new product launch."

A closed-ended question might be: "Do you agree with launching the product on 16 July?"

The important thing about this kind of inquiry is that it benefits both sides of the dialogue; the leader doing the questioning and the follower or the stakeholder who is being listened to. The questioner is getting the information he or she needs and the follower gets the sense that their ideas and experiences are important.

It's not that closed-ended questions are never called for. But the problem is that you're unlikely to learn much from asking them. They don't lead into a dialogue, and they're often a dead-end.

According to Niels Van Quaquebeke, professor of leadership and organizational behavior at Kühne Logistics University, and originator of the term "respectful inquiry" as it applies to this particular method of questioning, the employee or other stakeholder is being prodded to clarify their own thoughts and needs. He notes that "respectful inquiry principally satisfies the basic psychological needs for competence, relatedness, and autonomy".

Unfortunately, as he comments, the technique is as extremely rare as it is extremely valuable.[7]

In a sense, the mere fact that you have gone through this process with an open mind will draw people to you, make them see you as part of their support network, and make it more likely that your strategy will be a success. If you haven't carried out this initial communicating step your strategy will, inevitably, fail in execution.[8]

Who do you tell, and when?

Probably the best communicator of strategy over the last 20 years has been Southwest Airways. To the question of when do you communicate your strategy to your employees, its answer is: *immediately you've decided on it* (they always go through the asking and listening stage first).

Southwest, along with Toyota, believes that transparency in this area is the key to success, and for both companies, it has been. Transparency is the key to trust and trust is the key to making a strategy work. You don't have to put the new strategy into practice immediately, but you must communicate your intentions immediately.

Professional service firms have found that the same transparency works for them. According to Simon Bevan, a senior partner in the UK division of the giant global accountancy firm Grant Thornton, the benefit of this approach is that people in the business at all levels act like owners of a shared enterprise.

Of course, there are times when the value of secrecy is greater than the value of transparency, and this is certainly true of the strategy-formulation stage of the process. But once the new strategic direction has been decided, there is no benefit in secrecy, and a huge benefit in transparency.

The "how" of communicating change

So, you've done the preliminary listening and you've worked out the details of your strategy. You're going to be transparent and you're now going to give the news to the workforce.

Obviously how you communicate any fundamental change depends very largely on the size and cultural context of the organization. Despite this, there are several fundamentals that apply in any situation and in any culture.

In a large, or even mid-sized, organization, communicating the strategy one-on-one with every employee is probably not possible. Some sort of electronic medium must be used – but remember McLuhan's hamburger. Humans are designed for face-to-face interaction, so whatever medium of communication you use it should be as close to face-to-face as possible. The meat of what you are saying will be more readily accepted if it has the right buns and fixings. In human terms that means it must involve as many senses as possible. The human brain uses each sense to judge the trustworthiness of the communicator – the tone of voice, the facial and body movements, even the pheromones being given off.

The preferred means of communicating a strategy to your stake-holders – based on human design-specs – are given below. Their relative strength in engendering trust is graded on a 0-10 scale. Ten points is best.

1. Best method, vital in a small organization, is in person, face-to-face. All senses in play, plus participation. Most trust (10 points).

2. Small group meetings with influencers who will communicate the strategy more widely. Good in conjunction with other explanatory tools such as interactive webinars. All senses activated at some level. Possible high trust (9 points).

3. Town hall-style meetings. These work, but only if they are very interactive. All senses in play to some extent, obviously pheromones not so much so. Trust depends on the level of interaction. With high participation as possible (8 points).

4. Close-up interactive webinar or similar. Sight and sound plus participation. Possible good trust (7 points).

5. Non-interactive VC. Sight, sound. No participation. Some trust possible (3 points).

6. Interactive audio conference. Sound and participation. Some trust possible (3 points).

7. Non-interactive audio conference. Sound. No participation. Little trust possible (1 point).

8. Text, email etc. Maximum distrust (minus 8 points).[9]

The big take-aways

1. Listen mindfully to your stakeholders before you begin to evolve your strategy.
2. Ask open-ended questions.
3. Tell your employees as soon as you have decided on your strategy.
4. Communicate, when possible, face-to-face.

References

1. Baumeister, R. F., Twenge, J. M. and Nuss, C. K. (2002) "Effects of social exclusion on cognitive processes: Anticipated aloneness reduces intelligent thought", *Journal of Personality and Social Psychology*, 83:4 pp. 817-827.
2. Jones, P. (2016) *Communicating Strategy*, Routledge, New York.
3. McLuhan, M. (1964) *Understanding Media*, Mcgraw-Hill, New York.
4. Gregersen, H. (2017) "Bursting the CEO Bubble", *Harvard Business Review*, March 2017.
5. Wolvin, A. D. and Coakley C. G. (2009) "A survey of the status of listening training in some fortune 500 corporations," *Communication Education*, 40:2, 152-164.
6. Wolvin, A. D. and Coakley, C. G. (2012) "Listening Education in the 21st Century", *International Journal of Listening*, pp. Vol. 14, 143-152.
7. Van Quaquebeke, N. and Felps, W. (2016) "Respectful Inquiry: A Motivational Account of Leading Through Asking Questions and Listening," *Academy of Management Journal*, 43:1 (first pub. online).
8. Jorritsma, P. L. and Wilderom, C. (2012) "Failed culture change aimed at more service provision: a test of three agentic factors," *Journal of Organizational Change Management*, 25:3 pp. 364-391.
9. This grading system is one we have used for three years and is based on a number of studies e.g. Hill, S. N. et al (2009) "Organizational context and face-to-face interaction: Influences on the development of trust and collaborative behaviors in computer-mediated groups", *Organizational Behavior and Human Decision Processes*, 108:2, pp.187-201 and our own research. See also Gorman, C. K. (2015) "Why You Are More Successful in Face-To-Face Meetings", *Forbes*, 25 October 2015.

Chapter 10:
Getting buy-in to change

Getting buy-in to change is getting buy-in to you. This buy-in is far more important for acceptance and implementation than the intellectual beauty of your strategy.

Humans are averse to change. We don't change quickly and if we try to, we don't change permanently. If you go on a crash diet and succeed in swiftly losing a lot of pounds, the net result will generally be that the kilos, pounds, and inches will come back – sometimes more rapidly than they went off.

Change of almost any kind goes through the same neural mechanism as physical and emotional pain. Our neurogenetic system sees it as a threat, something to be avoided. Yet every strategy is essentially about change, often radical change.

Successful change is about influence, it's about individual relationships, and it's about belonging. A successful change manager must understand and utilize all three aspects. It's also about him or her realizing that there is a difference between change in beliefs, mindsets, and assumptions, which can be very difficult, and behavioral change, which can be much easier.

An astute change manager does not try to directly change a person's mindset – their beliefs and their assumptions about themselves and the world – but their behaviors. He or she gives the person a relationally safe space to experiment with behavioral change and praises them for trying.

A parent does this when their offspring comes last in a race. A poor parent will scold the child for not trying hard enough. A more enlightened one will say something like: "I am so proud of the way that you kept running, even when you were at the back of the field and might just have given up".

The child's reaction to the first parent might well be "I can't win, where's the point in trying". The reaction to the second will probably be increased effort to get more praise, and an openness to behavioral change. Dopamine, the reward neurochemical that is triggered by praise, also opens the brain to learning.

The neurogenetics of influence

To understand where we're going with this, remember that a human being at any given time is made up of three elements, and each one is involved in the process of change or stasis. The three elements are what we call the *what* of a person, the *who* of a person, and the *where* of that person.

The *what* of a person is essentially our neurobiology, our physiology, and our genetics. These dictate many of our actions, our moods and our beliefs, and the majority of our decisions – even, to a large degree, the strategy we are trying to persuade our stakeholders to buy into. Most of the "what" is immutable, but by no means all.

Our genes are divided into three types. The major division is between what are called "protein-coding genes," which are the active ones that influence almost every facet of our body and mind. There are only about 20,000 of them (we used to think there were millions) so each of them is very busy controlling many aspects of our physical and mental being. Protein-coding sequences account for only a very small fraction of the genome (approximately 1.5 percent), and the rest is associated with non-coding RNA molecules, regulatory DNA sequences, LINEs, SINEs, introns, and sequences for which as yet no function has been determined.[1] The protein encoding genes are themselves divided into two types – what are called "hard" and "soft" genes. Hard genes govern our height, our hair color, our eye color, our susceptibility to certain diseases such as Alzheimer's, several cancers and so forth. Mostly these are passed on through DNA from an individual's parentage.

Soft genes are also passed on through DNA; however, they can be influenced in their "expression" (the way they operate) by factors outside the body – if, for example, we force someone to live or work in a polluted environment,[2] or one floor too high off the ground (over five stories).[3] We can influence these soft genes and therefore a person's mindset and behavior, through the relationship we have with them and the context that we create for them.

Daniel Goleman in his book *Social Intelligence*[4] shows that every inter-action with another person or group of people changes the way our soft genes express. We change each other through our moods, the language we use, even our facial expressions. Another person's smile can make us feel happy or safe, their frown can cause us to feel uneasy or agitated.

The success of implementing your strategy depends very largely on the way you are able to alter the expression of a person's soft genes. Do this in the right way and the person – or people – will become committed to you and hence to your strategy.

The *who* of a person is essentially everything that has happened to that individual since conception. Largely this is their prenatal experience (through the mood of their mother during pregnancy), their parenting, their schooling, and their childhood relationships, but also the social context they were raised in.

In our adult life we tend to seek out relationships with people who are, in some way, like our parents or other childhood authority figures. This is called adult attachment. We see our parents as ideals – no matter how unideal they might have been. If we had an insecure relationship with our parents, we will probably seek out relationships with people who may abandon us – or we may (unconsciously) push people into abandoning us. In the workplace this dynamic can be seen in employees who adopt behaviors that are almost certain to get them fired.

On the other hand, if the attachment to our parents was secure, we will tend to seek out secure relationships – including with our managers, leaders, and family. If you, as a leader, can offer the safety that a secure relationship offers and if you can role-model the kind of caring for your followers that good parents should, then the acceptance of your strategic plan by them will be almost automatic.

Just like a child seeks safety by forging a close relationship with his or her parents through doing what they suggest, so your employees will use the same techniques to find safety in their relationship with you.

But even if an employee has a history of insecure attachments, you can create a supportive context for them to work in by emphasizing commonality, and a secure relationship through role modeling good parenting skills such as listening and clearly communicating expectations. In this way you will get the commitment to you that is essential for implementing your strategy.

Finally, the *where* of a person is the context that a person is in. It's the lighting, the office layout, the relational atmosphere (such as the management style of supervisors and any bullying or harassment), the level of stress, overwork, and job security. All of these interact with the what and the who and influence the employee in a number of ways – some positive and some obviously negative.

If you want to get the best out of your employees by using the who and the where, you will:

- Adopt a transformational (people-centered) leadership style;
- Role model the kind of work and relational behaviors you would like to see your followers adopt;
- Remember that you are a parental figure so it's important for you to behave like a good parent;
- Do not adopt an office layout where people feel uncomfortable, or lack privacy, or are competing for space – as can sometimes be the case with hot desking, for example;
- Have as much natural light as possible and make sure that everyone has an outlook that includes some aspect of nature; and
- Crack down hard on any bullying or harassment.

These fairly simple steps will make sure that human design specs will be working in your favor as you seek to get your strategy accepted and implemented.

The how-to of influencing

As we've mentioned several times in this book, human decision-making is not based on facts or reasoning. We are not rational animals. Our decisions are influenced by the non-rational elements that make up our what, who, and where.

But more than that, we make decisions on the basis of emotions, particularly fear and the expectation of reward. Many researchers used to be convinced that fear was the greatest persuader, and that therefore threat of harm – job loss, lack of promotion, salary reduction etc. – would be the best persuasion technique.[5]

We now know that's not true. Fear can be used to persuade, but only in the short term,[6] and since almost every strategic initiative is a long term enterprise, the promise of reward is far more effective. But not every reward is equal. The most powerful and longest lasting is relational reward.

To be an effective persuasion tool, the relationship promised must be one offering physical or emotional support, or both. Recent research has shown that a human being's primary need is to be surrounded by a network of supportive relationships. This is largely because humans – unlike most other mammals – have no effective inbuilt means of defense. We can't out-run most of our natural predators, we can't climb trees to escape, we have no camouflage, and as defensive weaponry our claws and our teeth are pitiful. Our curiosity and our inventiveness led us to devise clubs and axes, spears and, much later, bows and arrows. However, even these are fairly ineffective against an elephant, a pair of hunting lions, a snake or a pack of jackals.

Our only means of defense is to be in the company of other humans who will have our backs. And that was the case for over four million years – since the days of Lucy and her Australopithecus kin.[7] That need for communal support is at the very heart of our DNA – right up there with the need for sustenance, shelter, and reproduction.

Therefore, commitment to you as a leader, and to your strategy, depends on your being able – through your actions – to convince your followers that you are able and willing to protect them. That is relational support. You and your employees must have a mutual satisfaction of needs – they will satisfy your need for obedience in getting your strategy fulfilled and in return you give them the promise of protection.

But how do you evidence your willingness to protect? Simple – you use praise and acknowledgement. If you give someone praise or acknowledgement – especially publicly – they will be more likely to feel that they are special to you, that they won't be abandoned by you, and you will protect them. The reward neurochemicals that we mentioned earlier – dopamine and oxytocin – will see to that. But, of course, you have to follow through.

There are three types of praise and it is necessary to be skillful at using all of them.

The first, and the most commonly used, is the one we call "what praise". This is for when someone has done something special, such as won a new client, exceeded his or her sales targets, designed a new product or, of course, come up with a new strategy. If you don't praise or acknowledge an achievement, you are giving the person a message that they don't matter to you and therefore why should you matter to them? A "what praise" message must be specific and be seen to matter to you. An email saying, "Well done, team!" is useless since it is neither specific nor personal.

The second kind of praise is "how praise". This is praise for the effort a person put in, the innovation they used, their ingenuity. It's about how they went about the task. Whereas "what" is about succeeding, "how" is about going out of their way and about trying rather than triumphing. It is the praise you use when you want to instill a learning message. If you praise someone for how they did something they will do it that way again in order to get the praise reward.

You can use this reward when you've suggested that they try a new way of doing something or attempt a more difficult task, and they do so. Even if they don't succeed, you praise the effort. In implementing a new strategy this is a great persuasion tool.

Finally, there is the most powerful persuasion tool of all – "who praise". It makes use of both of the brain's main neurochemical reward systems. Unfortunately, it is not only the most powerful form of praise, it is also the least used! This is about acknowledging the relationship with the other person and can be seen through phrases such as "I really appreciate having you on my team", "I feel I always have your support", and "You're always fun to be around".

Praise, good role-modelling actions, and being an understanding "parent" to your followers will get the buy-in you need for successful implementation of your strategy.

A sense of belonging

To humans, belonging is a fluid concept that includes a sense of tribe – belonging to a group – and a sense of autonomy over a space or territory. In terms of getting buy-in to your initiative both are important.

As we have mentioned, a business or any organization is a tribe. People come to work primarily to relate, to be a member of the tribe, to belong in that sense of the word. If they feel they belong they will work hard and creatively to support the tribe – just as hunter-gatherers did, when the strength of the tribe was their safety.

To belong is a human's strongest drive. Our greatest fear is isolation, rejection and abandonment. Therefore, to get buy-in to a strategy you must be able to convince employees that the new strategy will increase the strength of the tribe. But there is a catch – in a mid-size or large firm people's sense of belonging is not to the business or organization as a whole. Rather it's to smaller sections of it – their work group, their department, the people on their floor, their silo. It's to these that they relate on a day-to day basis. That's where they look to for safety, for understanding and for belonging. It's these groups that they will work to preserve and to strengthen.

Each of these sectors will have their own needs and, in many ways, their own cultures, which include the commonalities that they have acquired over time.

If your plan seems to endanger these clusters, the members will actively or passively work to undermine it. The new strategy may be good for the company, but in most cases your employees don't care about the company, only their own small part of it.

Therefore, you need to target your communications about strategy to these groups and their concerns and needs as well as to the organization as a whole.

The other aspect of belonging is to territory. In human science terms, territory is space that an individual can exercise autonomy over or feels they can control. This can be as large as a hunting or foraging area or as small as their own desk with their own things on it.

There are many benefits to activity-based workplaces (ABW), which feature hot-desking and no sense of territorial ownership, and similar layouts, but one of the great drawbacks is the loss of a sense of control over a space – an individual territory.[8] To this can be added the loss of a sense of belonging in the tribal sense of the word, since teams no longer necessarily work together, no longer share space. There is no individual, or tribal, territory.

This can lead to a feeling of a lack of belonging to the organization. Indeed, another drawback of ABW is that, after a short honeymoon period, employees realize that the main benefactor of the layout is the organization's bottom-line – and their hostility to the organization as a whole increases.[9]

Under these circumstances a change initiative of any kind – especially a strategy that will involve further disruption – has little chance of success. A leader saddled with an unpopular office layout (whether ABW or open plan) must work that much harder to create a sense of unity among teams and departments and increase their sense of a larger commonality.

The big take-aways

1. Practice being a good parent to your employees.
2. Use the neurogenetics of the "what", "who" and "where".
3. Add the reward power of the "what," "how," and "who" praise and you're sure to get the commitment you need to implement your strategy.

References

1. International Human Genome Sequencing Consortium (February 2001). "Initial sequencing and analysis of the human genome," *Nature*. 409, 6, 822, pp. 860-921.
2. Lelieveld, J. et al (2019) "Cardiovascular disease burden from ambient air pollution in Europe reassessed using novel hazard ratio functions," *European Heart Journal*, EZH 135.
3. Gifford, R. (2007) "The Consequences of Living in High-Rise Buildings," *Architectural Science Review*, 50:1.
4. Goleman, D. (2006) *Social Intelligence*, Bantam, NY.
5. "Fear as a strategy: effects and impact within the organization," *Journal of European Industrial Training*, Vol. 22, Issue 3, pp.113-127.
6. Dambe, M. and Moorad, F. (2008) "From Power to empowerment: a paradigm shift in leadership," 22:3, p. 575.
7. Kimbel, W. H., Rak, Y. and Johanson, D. C. (2004) *The Skull of Australopithecus afarensis*, OUP, Oxford.
8. Wohlers, C. and Hertel, G. (2017): "Choosing where to work at work – towards a theoretical model of benefits and risks of activity-based flexible offices," *Ergonomics*, 60:4, pp. 467-486
9. Parker, L. (2016), "From scientific to activity based office management: a mirage of change", *Journal of Accounting and Organizational Change*, 12:2, pp. 177-202.

Chapter 11:
Building trust in the strategy and the leadership

As we said earlier, a large majority of employees do not trust their immediate supervisors, and even less their senior management. Very few managers of an enterprise of any size really have the trust of their staff.

Scientifically, we know the elements that make up trust and how to attain the trust of other people. It's what we call the "5Cs" of trust. Without these there can be no trust and without trust there is no successful strategy. The application of any strategic initiative depends on a deep trusting relationship between management and the workforce.

The five Cs of trust

The five Cs of trust in any organizational (and most other) relationships are:

1. Commonality. The more you have in common with another person or group, the more they will trust you. You become part of their tribe and the greater the sense of tribe, the greater the trust;[1]

2. Consistency. This element combines several ideals – predictability, walking the talk, and doing what you say you will;

3. Competence, or good judgement and expertise. This is the extent to which a leader is well-informed and knowledgeable. They must understand the technical aspects of the work as well as have a depth of experience. They must perceptibly be able to fulfil their promises;

4. Care for the other person. Sometimes this is called "benevolent concern". It means that you are prepared to go out of your way for the other person, often in ways that involve self-sacrifice; and

5. Communication. This means both frequent and face-to-face communication. We need to communicate frequently to achieve trust and to allow the other person to judge us using as many senses as possible (like any mammal we need all of our senses to fully establish trust).[2]

If any one of these elements is missing then trust, even if it has existed before, becomes very fragile and can be easily lost.

Commonality: Making a tribe, not just a workforce

Human beings naturally try to find commonality – something to unite around. If there is nothing, then they tend to break into mutually hostile groups whose unity is their opposition to the other groups.

The essence of a tribe – as we mentioned earlier – is that the individuals in a group have a substantial number of things in common. This, of course, becomes a culture. But commonality can be found in context – we live in this area, we work for the same firm, we go to the same school, our offices, or workstations, are on the same floor. It can arise from shared experience – we met in the same traffic jam, our lives were disrupted by the same power failure, we were out-bid at the same auction, we both attended the same rally. Commonality can also include broader elements such as nationality, ethnicity, religion (for example, the most profitable law firm in Australia is made up predominately of lawyers of one particular faith), or even gender (for example, banks run for and by women in India and Pakistan).

Once a sense of commonality has been established, people will see themselves as part of a tribe (in our modern urban society we can belong to many tribes at any one time – our home tribe, our sports club, and so forth). We become loyal to our tribes and their survival and prospering becomes very important to us. We work harder for our tribe and will be readier to defend it (which is why businesses are so keen to increase their employees' engagement levels). The more your people share a sense of commonality, the easier it is for them to feel safe enough to change.

If you can show that you and your people have a great deal in common, they will be more likely to follow your directives and implement your strategy.

The danger is that if you and they have few things in common, they may well unite around opposition to you and what you are trying to achieve.

Showing consistency of good behavior

People will trust you and your strategy if you:

- Consistently behave in the same way;
- Are a role model for good behavior;
- Do what you say you will and act as you require others to behave; and

- Always strive to go above and beyond what needs to be done.

As a leader, or a manager at any level, it's important to bear in mind that people want to be able to mentally prepare for working with you each morning. They don't want surprises. It's important to be consistently good in your behavior. Some researchers have gone as far as to say that if you can't be consistently good, then at least be consistently bad. Trust is destroyed very quickly if you're unpredictable – it gives people no solid ground on which to build a relationship with you.

Building a sense of competence

In terms of building trust, competence has a number of meanings, including demonstrating:

- Good judgement and expertise;
- The capability to fulfil the function you're allotted; and
- The ability to fulfil your promises.[3]

Oddly enough, humans are forward-looking animals and we tend not to look back to the past for our guide to the future. This can be most obviously seen in the case of the "battered wife syndrome". When we were in private psychotherapy practice in New York many years ago we were frequently confronted with clients whose spouses had just physically attacked them. If it was a woman we would suggest that a safe house was the best place for them to go to. Sometimes they did but, even then, they were more than likely to return to the batterer.

"He (she) has changed," the client would say. "He (she) is sorry and promises not to hit me again."

"And you believe that?"

"This time it's different."

It's always different. We find the same thing in politics, with the office bully, with the serial abuser or offender. We dismiss the past and look for a rosy future. We see and give precedence to the "perception" that this time the promises will be kept.

It's for this reason that trust needs to have not just one of the five Cs satisfied, but all of them. To be a trusted leader – and therefore a successful strategist – you have to be above average in all of these elements of trust.[4]

Care, or benevolent concern

Trust is an issue because people are often self-centered. A leader is trusted because his or her followers believe that he or she has their back, will fight for them, will take a personal risk for them.

Business professor Robert Hurley in his seminal 2006 *HBR* article "The Decision to Trust" says:

> *"The manager who demonstrates benevolent concern – who shows his employees that he will put himself at risk for them – engenders not only trust but also loyalty and commitment."*

Unless someone is willing to take that risk to keep you safe, to meet your needs, there is really no reason to trust them. If you are asking your employees to take a risk for you by implementing your strategy, then you must ask yourself: what risk are you willing to take for them?

Most leaders that we have met in industry – particularly in large corporations or firms – are very unwilling to take a personal risk. Undoubtedly this is one main reason why 80 percent of strategic initiatives fail.

Take, for example, a large law firm in Australia. The management pushed a strategy that meant that support staff, solicitors, and partners were constantly being asked to produce more income with fewer resources. The problems, according to the regulator, SafeWork NSW, involved staff (lawyers and others) overworking with insufficient rest breaks and the absence of policies to manage worker fatigue. This led to drug and supplement abuse as staff tried to keep themselves alert.[5]

Would the founder and CEO of the firm push himself to that extent? Who knows, but, like many other CEOs, probably not.

Communication, *the more the better*

As Hurley says:

> *"Because trust is a relational concept, good communication is critical. Not surprisingly, open and honest communication tends to support the decision to trust, whereas poor (or no) communication creates suspicion. Many organizations fall into a downward spiral – miscommunication causes employees to feel betrayed, which leads to a greater breakdown in communication and, eventually, outright distrust."*

Over the last decade and a half since that was written we have learned a lot more about the science of communication. In particular we have found that face-to-face and in-person communication vastly increases trust, while electronic means such as email actually decrease it. This is because we communicate through facial cues and body language as much, if not more, than we do through words.

For example, we watch for tiny twitches in facial muscles, especially around the eyes and mouth, which happen when we lie.

We also rely on our sense of smell. A pheromone is a chemical substance produced and released into the environment by mammals and insects, affecting the behavior or physiology of others of its species. Pheromones are meant for communication. For example, oxytocin, the "love," "bonding," and "trust" neurochemical and pheromone, signals both desire and trust. It is difficult to really trust someone without being able to (subconsciously at least) detect the scent. Scenting oxytocin tells you that the other person trusts you and thus allows you to relax and trust them.

While the above indicators seem to make some kind of sense, others may come across as unreasonable but affect us none the less. For example, we tend to trust people more if they have deep voices, if they are tall, and if we find them attractive.

Be that as it may, the more senses we bring to an interaction, the more trust is engendered. The fewer sensual clues we have, the less we trust. This makes it important for you to deliver the message about your strategy in person or through someone who really believes in it.

Fear creates distrust
Hurley also said:

> "A general rule to remember: The higher the stakes, the less likely people are to trust. If the answer to the question 'What's the worst that could happen?' isn't that scary, it's easier to be trustful. We have a crisis of trust today in part because virtually nobody's job is truly secure, whereas just a generation ago, most people could count on staying with one company throughout their careers."[6]

Since Hurley wrote that, things have become much "scarier". The idea of holding onto a permanent job is much more fanciful, the threat of joblessness much more real. The most that many people can hope for is an Uber-type gig, whether you drive a car, or are a banker, an accountant, or a lawyer.

Many recent studies have shown that innovation, adaptability, change, and flexibility all only really happen when people feel safe.[7] This applies to your strategy because, as we've said earlier, you need the trust of your staff, suppliers, and customers. Each of these, in their separate ways, are going to be asked to do or believe something different – to take a physical or cognitive risk. To do so they must feel that your strategy will ultimately increase their sense of safety.

It's important to find ways to temper the apparent risk inherent in the situation and invest time in finding ways to raise comfort levels.

Remember that comfort and safety lie in relationships. Find ways to preserve and strengthen relational security. Trust is essentially a relationship statement. Someone's willingness to support or implement your strategy is a statement of trust; it's "I feel safe enough in the context of my relationship with you to take a chance, to put myself at risk".

The big take-aways

1. Bear in mind the 5Cs of trust.
2. Deliver the message about your strategy in person.
3. Do as much as you can to reduce the level of fear and uncertainty.
4. Find out what showing concern for your employees means to them.
5. Develop commonality with those who will implement your strategy.

References

1. For more on this see Murray, B. and Fortinberry, A. (2013) "Rethinking Leadership Training," *Effective Executive*, 16:3 pp. 40-46.
2. Shichida Y. et al (2013) *Evolution and Senses*, Springer, Tokyo.
3. Oliveira, T. et al (2017) "Modelling and testing consumer trust dimensions in e-commerce," *Computers in Human Behavior*, 21:2017, pp. 153-164.
4. For more on this see Zenger, J. and Folkman, J. (2019) "The Three Elements of Trust," *HBR*, February 2019.
5. Garvey, P. (2019) "SafeWork NSW probes Gilbert + Tobin over drug use," *The Australian*, 1 June 2019.
6. Hurley, R. F. (2006) "The Decision to Trust," *HBR*, September 2006.
7. Martinez-Sanchez, A. et al (2011) "The Dynamics of Labor Flexibility: Relationships between Employment Type and Innovativeness," *Journal of Management Studies*, 48:4, pp. 715-736.

Chapter 12:
Getting it all right

When we began interviewing for this book, we spoke to David Brown, currently group CEO of Australia's Solgen Energy Group. We asked him what he thought was the main reason that his strategies worked more than others. He said:

> *"I create a safe environment where people are respected. If people believe that I care about them they feel safe enough to be brave. It's all about relationships. A good CEO is continuously under scrutiny. His followers are constantly asking themselves: 'Can I trust him? Is this strategy just for him and the shareholders?' Your people will work to implement your strategy if they feel they will benefit. Strategy must be about people."*

It's the relationships, stupid!

All of the successful strategic leaders we spoke to underscored that simple message. For example, Mark Rigotti, the CEO of Herbert Smith Freehills, said:

> *"Strategy is made up of people's ideas. If they can see their own thinking in your strategy, then you'll get their buy-in."*

Tristram Carfrae, the deputy chairman of Arup, also reiterated:

> *"For a strategy to be successful you have to have enough voices at the table so that people see that it works for them. Strategic decision-making is not a top-down exercise. Consultation and decision-making at Arup is both bottom-up and top-down. Strategic change is slow and people-centered."*

Strategic thought and strategic implementation are all about relationships and that's because humans are all about relationships. Any organization is in the end just an excuse for relationships – that's in our DNA.

Strategies fail mostly because relationships fail. To understand why this happens you must understand how human beings work. You must understand human design specs.

Humans are designed to seek out a nexus of supportive relationships. We seek safety and in doing so we are not really concerned that much with facts and reasoning. You don't win people over to your ideas or your strategy by trying to persuade them with data. Rather, you win them over by getting them invested in their relationship with you – essentially by making them feel that you will keep them safe, by showing them that they can trust you, and that you have a purpose within which they can find meaning.

Humans are tribal animals. They will work hard to protect their tribe. To have a successful implementation of your strategy you have to create sufficient commonality within your workplace that it becomes a tribe to defend, and to show your people that your strategy will help to preserve the tribe and thus keep them safe.

Don't rely on assumptions
Humans are terrible at making correct assumptions. About 70 percent of all our assumptions and beliefs are wrong. Worse, 90 percent of our assumptions about other people are, to a large extent, wrong. Never assume that you know what your people want or need. Always ask. More importantly, you don't really understand yourself. Your own assumptions and biases will ensure that you will misjudge your own strategy.

Most leaders believe – often subconsciously – that they are right and fail to listen to those voices that indicate that this may not be the case. You must learn to check your own assumptions, and see what your previous decisions and actions indicate your beliefs, biases, and assumptions to be. Only then are you ready to come to decisions regarding strategy.

Work on getting people to trust you
Your strategy will only work if people trust you. Before you begin to design or implement a new strategy, work on the five Cs of trust. Any change requires relational trust to be implemented. An announcement from on high will not motivate support – more often it'll spark opposition and lead to failure.

There is a right and a wrong way to lead for strategic success
Not every leadership style is consistently right for strategic success. Overall, only one is – transformational leadership. Make sure that you

understand what this is all about and practice it before you launch into a change program.

The main elements of transformational leadership are:

- Idealized influence – the leader is a role model and behaves the way he/she wants employees to behave;
- Inspirational motivation – the leader presents a vision for the future of the organization to inspire employees;
- Individualized consideration – the leader develops one-on-one relationships to help employees reach their potential; and
- Intellectual stimulation – the leader encourages employees to be creative and challenges them to go above and beyond.

What a transformational leader does is:

- Emphasizes intrinsic motivation and positive development of followers;
- Raises awareness of moral standards;
- Highlights important priorities;
- Fosters higher moral maturity in followers;
- Creates an ethical climate (shares values, sets high ethical standards);
- Encourages followers to look beyond self-interests to the common good;
- Promotes cooperation and harmony;
- Uses authentic, consistent means;
- Uses persuasive appeals based on mutual support;
- Provides individual coaching and mentoring for followers;
- Appeals to the ideals of followers; and
- Allows freedom of choice for followers.

Make sure your strategy aligns with your purpose

Your employees will only work hard to implement your strategy if they believe it has some purpose other than making money or earning profits. A recent study by the Gallup Organization found that only 27 percent of employees strongly believe in their company's values or purpose, and less than half strongly agree that they know what their organization stands for and what makes it different.

Leaders should worry about that. An actionable purpose has a positive effect on everything a company does. Such a focus unites and touches every stakeholder, including customers, employees, regulators, legislators, the media, and influencers. These are just the ones who are going to make your strategy succeed or fail.[1]

That's all folks!

If you follow the recommendations in this book and make sure that you follow the guidelines that our design specs dictate, then your strategy will have an 80 percent chance of succeeding rather than an 80 percent chance of failing. Best of luck – let us know how it goes. We're at www.fortinberrymurray.com.

Reference

1. Robinson, J. (2019) "The Future of Your Workplace Depends on Your Purpose," *Gallup at Work*, 24 May 2019.